Fight Direction

FOR STAGE AND SCREEN

Fight Direction

FOR STAGE AND SCREEN

WILLIAM HOBBS

*Forewords by **Laurence Olivier** and **Roman Polanski***

Heinemann

A & C Black · London

First published 1980 by Barrie & Jenkins as *Stage Combat*
This edition first published 1995
A & C Black (Publishers) Limited
35 Bedford Row, London WC1R 4JH

ISBN 0-7136-4022-7

© 1995, 1980, William Hobbs

Published simultaneously in the USA by Heinemann
A Division of Reed Publishing (USA) Inc.
361 Hanover Street
Portsmouth, NH 03801-3912
Offices and Agents throughout the world

Distributed in Canada by Reed Books Canada,
75 Clegg Road, Markham, Ontario L6G 1A1

ISBN 0-435-08680-4

CIP catalogue records for this book are available
from the British Library and the Library of Congress.

Typeset in 10½ on 12pt Linotron Sabon by
Rowland Phototypesetting Limited,
Bury St Edmunds, Suffolk.
Printed in Great Britain by Biddles Limited,
Guildford, Surrey.

Some of the material in this book is taken from
Techniques of the Stage Fight by William Hobbs,
published by Studio Vista Limited in 1967.

Contents

for Janet, Laurence and Edwin

also
my brother-in-law
John Riley
in fond memory

Foreword

I have enjoyed working with William Hobbs twice. Both occasions were truly memorable. His contributions to *Pirates* and *Macbeth* were impressive, adding reality, dramatic tension and visual excitement. I often think of the fights in armour he staged for *Macbeth*. Although one critic compared the scene to being like Nervo and Knox in tin cans, Hobbs gave me a completely new effect – a thudding blade and body bashing reality – something that, strangely, had not been done before.

Bill and I had agreed from the start on the look of the fights for *Macbeth*. I didn't want anything theatrical. The reality of period sword fighting was more like a brawl in an alley. I liked to see snarled up, contorted bodies in unusual positions. He once suggested and we used an upside down victim lifted up with his legs over the attacker's shoulders.

I recall Bill coming to visit me in London to discuss *Pirates*. He asked me how many fight scenes would be in the film. I could not resist teasing him. I answered 'one, the whole film is one long fight'.

The William Hobbs sword fight sequences which have graced so many films are the result of long and complex activity. While he is noted for inventively choreographing exciting and dramatically credible action, he is also responsible for training the actors and the stuntmen who have to perform his choreography of mortal-appearing action. Behind the scenes he is a gifted teacher, a psychiatrist and a coach. He instructs with the same finesse he brings to his duelling. He charms, coaxes and cajoles toward steady improvement. I have frequently watched him create a swordsman by convincing the actor he was far more adept than he was and then miraculously making him better. He stimulates and encourages his pupils to work harder, longer and to keep giving that extra added bit more of themselves until they perform to his required standard. I admire his patience as well as the fact he never allows less than the best. Well, almost never. I remember during *Pirates*, I kept pestering him on how Walter Matthau was getting on. I wanted the best of him and for him. Bill was caught in the middle, because I knew Walter was pleading 'not too much work' and subtly mentioning again and again his triple-by-pass operation. 'We won't tell Roman' Walter conspired. Bill completely understood what was required and designed a few

7

simple routines which worked for the film and did not terribly tax Walter. But I knew all along what was happening between the two of them, and had enough confidence in Bill not to worry.

I recall another occasion on *Macbeth* when Bill was not only Fight Director but also playing as Young Siward. I needed a fine fighter for the less than demanding dramatic role. One day, Bill overslept and arrived late on the set to see me climbing into his armour. He was never late again, and fortunately I did not have to test myself as his double. I personally try to stay fit, but I would never truly imagine myself capable of fighting up to his uniquely high standard. He can stage fights, teach them and fight them better than anyone.

When Bill asked me to add a few words to his book, my first reaction was to decline because I felt Lord Olivier had already expressed all that I could ever say in his brilliant foreword. I try not to repeat myself in my films and I don't want to be redundant here. I learned that I would be expected only to update Bill's extraordinary work. He has accomplished so much since Larry passed away. Some of his credits during recent years are more eloquent testimonials to his skill than I could every say. *Dangerous Liaisons* with Glenn Close and Michelle Pfeiffer, *Cyrano de Bergerac* with Gerard Depardieu, Mel Gibson's *Hamlet* and *Rob Roy* with Liam Neeson and Jessica Lange.

What I can say without fear of contradiction is that William Hobbs has revolutionised swordplay on the screen. There is little in common between the swashbuckling bravura of Errol Flynn or my own *Macbeth* or Richard Lester's *The Three Musketeers* and Ridley Scott's *The Duellists*.

In all of those films, Hobbs achieved a new reality which evolved out of character and situation. He vitally contributes to the story telling with his precisely imagined action rather than plonking scene-stalling, sword waving action in the middle of a movie. Swashbuckling sword-whacking with little or no understanding of character continues in films today, but not in those in which Hobbs has been the Fight Director. He is an artist and I am proud of the work in the films we have done together. I am looking forward to future collaboration.

Roman Polanski

Original Foreword

'The Master of the Fence' is a splendid title, redolent of times when *le mot juste* was *le mot le plus splendide* or to be more vaudevillian:

> 'Those days of fame,
> When a Pansy was a flower
> And a Fanny was a name.'

Mr Hobbs has gone into his task with the extremest and most loving care and, I should guess, as thoroughly as can ever have been done.

I wish he had been born before I was, so that I could have had the benefit of such an abundance of advice and knowledge of technique.

My training and exercise in the art of fence has been largely grounded on the clockwork technique of 'one, two, three; two, one, four'; or 'bish, bash, bosh; bash, bosh, bish; no, no, no, you should not be doing bosh there, it is bash first, *then* bosh, *now* then, bosh, bash, bish, then *backhand* bosh'. This sounds idiotic enough but can be quite good if you look as if you really *mean* it, and use carefully practised variations of rhythm, also with a few escapes – I mean purposely narrow escapes – some surprises here and there and a frill or two, your little fight can look quite respectable.

I have always felt very strongly that a stage fight offered the actor a unique opportunity of winning the audience, as great almost as any scene, speech or action. That Shakespeare put it high in his estimation of stage effects is proclaimed by the amount of times he trustingly leaves it to this element to provide him with his dénouements, and this, as Mr Hobbs points out, for an audience commonly practised in the art and therefore shrewdly critical of the goings on.

There is a traditional paradox in reference to stage fights 'the safer the more dangerous'. Most accidents can be attributed to hesitancies and other symptoms of not wishing to hurt your opponent.

I have in my stage fighting life been more hurt than hurting, which would seem to absolve me in principle from this weakness, though in my mind's eye I see a couple of prone spectres of the past raising themselves upon a painful elbow aghast with speechless incredulity at my effrontery in making any such assertion.

I was first caused to muse upon these matters by an incident during *Romeo and Juliet* about Christmas-time 1935. I had hurt Geoffrey Toone quite badly in the Mercutio–Tybalt bout and the poor lad had to leave the cast for some weeks on account of his thumb *hanging by a thread*. The next evening I found myself squared up to the understudy – Harry Andrews no less. Each found something about his opponent that set his nostrils aquiver, if not his foot apawing and shrill neighing assailing the air. To each was flashed that instantaneous recognition of a kindred spirit. We both knew 'they' were going to get a good fight. From them on through the run no holds were barred and sparks flew like Japanese crackers and it was more up to the audience to defend itself as best it could rather than either of us.

We were using bucklers and hand-and-a-half hilted longish swords and hardly a performance went by that the tip of one of these did not go zinging out into the auditorium to be greeted by a female shriek, an outraged masculine snort of 'look here, I say', and a sobbing exit through one of the swing doors. How the management coped with it I shall never know.

Looking back over my career now, I see it as a long, a very long chapter of almost every imaginable kind of accident, which would seem to say that either I am a bad fighter or my rule of 'the safer the more dangerous' is a load of malarkey.

Without pausing for reflection I can think of:

1 broken ankle
2 torn cartilages (1 perforce yielding to surgery)
2 broken calf muscles
3 ruptured Achilles tendons
Untold slashes including a full thrust razor-edged sword wound in the
    breast (thrilling)
Landing from considerable height, scrotum first, upon acrobat's knee
Hanging by hand to piano wire 40 feet up for some minutes (hours?) on
    account of unmoored rope
Hurled to the stage from 30 feet due to faultily moored rope ladder
Impalement upon jagged ply cut-outs
Broken foot bone by standing preoccupied in camera track
Broken face by horse galloping into camera while looking through finder
Near broken neck diving into net
Several shrewd throws from horses including one over beast's head into
    lake
One arrow shot between shinbones
Water on elbow
Water pretty well everywhere
Hands pretty well mis-shapen now through 'taking' falls
Quite a few pretended injuries while it was really gout

Near electrocution through scimitar entering studio dimmer while backing away from unwelcome interview
Etc., etc., etc.

Not to mention injuries inflicted upon my colleagues. (Memories of R.R. as
Richmond, *sotto voce* but not unheard . . . 'Steady boy now', 'Easy fellow'
or 'You've got two today boy . . .' 'Merely venture to submit'.)
   Not to mention injuries inflicted upon my audiences.
   I could go on a great deal.
   Honourable scars? Well, I am not sure.
   But why introduce, with a chapter of accidents and mistakes, a text book
in which one is sure there are none?

Laurence Olivier

Acknowledgements

I should like to thank the following for their generous help in providing illustrations, photographs and information in the preparation of this book; Lesley Lindsay, Jack Barry, Henry Marshall, John Barton, Richard Bonehill, Bronwen Curry F.I.Chor., the Benesh Institute, Peter Boyes A.I.Chor., Cyril Brasher, Reg Amos, Raymond Mander, Joe Mitchenson, B. Barbier/Sygma and Artificial Eye (Distributors) for the photographs from *Cyrano de Bergerac* used on the front cover and in the book, Lucasfilm Ltd for the photograph from *Willow* used on the back cover, MGM for the UK rights and Dino De Laurentiis Communications/Paradise Films Inc. (© 1995 All rights reserved) for USA rights for use of the photograph from *Pirates* and my wife Janet.

Introduction

The experienced stage combat practitioner will see that many of the concepts and techniques outlined in this book are now common knowledge, but this wasn't the case in 1967 when I wrote the earlier version *Techniques of the Stage Fight*. There was, as far as I am aware, at that time only an older German manual on the subject, published in 1954 and titled *Buhnen-fectkunft* by I.E. Koch. This new revised version of mine is intended to reaffirm truths about the business which don't change, introduce the subject to new students and offer some recent thoughts from further experience gained. I hope it will be helpful to both arrangers and performers.

In bygone days, when duelling was commonplace, theatre audiences must have surely been critical of stage bouts when the real thing was not an unusual occurrence. Nowadays, when the public is unfortunately presented with all forms of violence, real and unreal, and a great deal of it, through the media, the job of presenting a staged fight is even more difficult. The main problem is how to give a production the effect of reality, while using only an acceptable level of simulated violence according to the requirements of the play. This level is a matter for each individual director and fight arranger to arrive at as responsible members of society, bearing in mind the particular concept of the piece and demands of the writer. It is not part of the aim of this book to enter into a debate on violence in the media, nor does it set out to deal with the special additional considerations to be taken into account in film and television. Much of what follows, however, in the way of basic analysis and preparation is equally applicable to stage, film or television. For example, the teaching of moves needs to be carried out with the same diligence whatever the form of preparation, but it is the selection of what is done which will often differ according to the varying requirements in the different forms of the media. The careful choice of detail that can be specially focused on by a close camera shot, and the use of special effects, are obvious examples of additional possibilities available in film making.

In films and television, unlike the stage, special stuntwork is possible where necessary, to assist the end result. The shooting of a television or film fight scene, after a proper rehearsal period, is often a one-day operation if that, which permits an actor to put his 'all' into a scene, in the knowledge

Rigid positions – oh, the aching legs! I wonder whether this couple would be able to move at all – although, judging by their finery, they might have been generally quite flamboyant movers.

Eric Mayne, Frederick Ross and Matheson Lang in The Prisoner of the Bastille, Lyceum Theatre, 1909.

that he can then forget it completely and go for a drink! On the stage, fights have to be performed effectively and safely night after night, which means that the actor cannot afford to become sloppy, or to take chances in an effort towards greater realism. Naturally, fights in any of the media have to be performed with safety, so in fact the same code of conduct – or rather, a disciplined attitude and method of working – is equally applicable to television, the stage or film. The main concern of this book is to offer overall guidelines to help in the business of tackling the preparation of a fight scene in whatever the media, with special focus given to the stage and with screen combat discussed separately.

The challenge of presenting a convincing, exciting and imaginative fight may on the face of it be a daunting prospect to the inexperienced, not unlike fitting together the pieces of a jigsaw puzzle. There are many moves and tricks however available to the arranger and actors. Thus, it is only when the various components, such as the creation and selection of moves which relate to character, the sharpening of the performer's skill and the proper forwarding of the story, are all put imaginatively together that the fight scene can be considered to work. Then we have the tricks of the trade – mostly stage, such as the simulation of the sound of a punch connecting, the secretion and showing of blood at the right moment, the masking from the audience of the moment of a blow's supposed connection and the sub-stitution of safe replica weapons in place of the real ones for a potentially dangerous move – all have their place in creating a few moments, or minutes, of theatrical illusion – or magic.

It is not my intention to formulate a rigid set of rules, for when it comes to arranging fights, each new play or production makes new demands that will involve new answers. The only rules which are always applicable are those combining safety and the illusion of reality. The few very fundamental moves which are explained later in the book are included not in order to teach, but to serve as illustrations of the care, precision and technique which have to be achieved, no matter how short and simple a sequence. To learn physical skills from a book, without training under a qualified tutor, is not I believe practicable. It is therefore my hope that what follows will act as a guide to the inexperienced, so that they can with professional help put their own ideas into operation more smoothly, this manual acting as a support to expert training. I also hope the book will help in promoting a professional attitude and way of thinking about the task of arranging and performing fight scenes, that will be useful in demonstrating the range of exciting possibilities and challenges which are open to fight directors, play directors and actors alike.

Henry Marston and Frederick Robinson in Henry IV Part I, *Sadler's Wells Theatre, 1846.*

An operatic feel to the famous duel, seemingly displaying a singular lack of urgency.

The duel scene from Hamlet *during Forbes Robertson's Farewell Season at the Theatre Royal, Drury Lane, 1913.*

'These foils have all a length?' Trouser length may be more the problem!

Frank Vosper, Dorothy Massingham, Colin Keith-Johnson, Robert Holmes and Guy Vivian in Hamlet *in modern dress, Kingsway Theatre, 1925.*

1.

Background

The further back one goes into history, the less is known about actual methods of fighting and how these were transferred into theatrical requirements. The interest and attention accorded to stage fights however is by no means new.

Going back to Victorian times, when the play demanded that the duel should be played, a number of well-known routines were often used, the most appropriate being selected according to the requirements of the play, but not specially created as nowadays. These were referred to in the profession of that time as 'The Square Eights', 'The Round Eights', 'The Glasgow Tens' (known in England as 'The Long Elevens'), and even one called 'The Drunk Combat'. All these routines were made up from a series of cuts – not cuts as we know them today, but rather whacks at the opponent's blade. These could be repeated as often as required all over the stage – again rather in the fashion that children play at sword-fighting with sticks; the elderly actor may just about recall these practices which were popular at one time.

The great Master of Fence of the mid-Victorian period was Felix Bertrand, who set many stage combats, including the duel between Tree and Fred Terry in *Hamlet*, Forbes Robertson's *Macbeth* and *Hamlet*, Ben Greet's *Nelson's Enchantress* and Wyndom's *Cyrano de Bergerac*; in fact, many of the leading actors of the day were pupils of Bertrand. Besides Tree, Forbes Robertson, Fred Terry and Ben Greet, these included Irving, Bancroft and Lewis Waller, as well as such writers as Thackeray and Dickens. Actors of the day considered the ability to fence an important asset, which must of course have made Bertrand's task much easier when it came to setting a fight. It is worth recording in this context that in the duel between Irving and Squire Bancroft in the play *The Dead Heart*, only the final hit was actually planned, so it seems fairly obvious that both men must have been experts with the blade, and as such would have been able to fence without trying for an actual hit – until the prepared and well-rehearsed final thrust. By today's standards, this may seem hardly a professional way of going about things,

A splendid lesson to reluctant actor/fighters. Looking at the picture, it is easy to appreciate why such plays as The Fencing Master's Daughter *were written for Victorian Theatre!*

Esmé Berringer, who died not long ago in her nineties, in the play — At the Point of the Sword, *1901.*

but this fight set all of London talking, and no wonder! It is even more remarkable when one learns that Irving was quite short-sighted – so short-sighted, in fact, that it is said that when he was playing a scene with an actress who was portraying a blind girl he accidentally dropped his glasses on the stage, and the 'blind' girl was the only one of the two would could 'see' to retrieve them! With such an affliction, it is almost incredible, and certainly to his credit (or luck), that he was able to perform such fights on the stage night after night, without any serious mishap.

Flying sparks were at this time considered an important feature of a fight. Irving was much enamoured of such effects, and would attach flints to the blade of his sword in order to achieve them. However, with the advent of electricity, in his pursuit of even greater 'fireworks', he actually had the weapons wired up to make sure they would constantly throw off sparks. Although it is not known whether any of his company was actually electrocuted, it wasn't long before he was using rubber insulation on the handles of the swords!

In the nineteenth and early twentieth century combats were a thriving and much-loved part of the theatrical scene, and many a bad play was devised as an excuse for 'a terrific combat'. The women too got in on the act – Miss Esmé Berringer called upon to fight in *At the Point of the Sword* was one example. Charles Dickens, himself a pupil of Bertrand, watched rehearsals of the combat in *Hamlet* between Fechter and Herman Vezin, and was sufficiently fascinated by stage fighting to include in *Nicholas Nickleby* a fight routine which was to be presented by the Crummles' Company. The fight must surely have been typical of the kind of combat relished by the audience who patronised productions by the many actor-managers of the day:

'Nicholas was prepared for something odd, but not for something quite so odd as the sight he encountered. At the upper end of the room, were a couple of boys, one of them very tall and the other very short, both dressed as sailors – or at least as theatrical sailors, with belts, buckles, pigtails, and pistols complete – fighting what is called in playbills a terrific combat, with two of those short broadswords with basket hilts which are commonly used at our minor theatres. The short boy had gained a great advantage over the tall boy, who was reduced to mortal strait, and both were overlooked by a large heavy man, perched against a corner of a table, who emphatically adjured them to strike a little more fire out of the swords, and they couldn't fail to bring the house down, on the very first night . . .

'. . . The two combatants went to work afresh, and chopped away until the swords emitted a shower of sparks: to the great satisfaction of Mr Crummles, who appeared to consider this a very great point indeed. The engagement commenced with about two hundred chops administered by the short sailor and the tall sailor alternately, without producing any particular result, until the short sailor was chopped down on one knee; but this was nothing to him, for he worked himself about on the one knee with the assistance of his left hand, and fought most desperately until the tall sailor chopped his sword out of his grasp. Now, the inference was, that the short sailor, reduced to this extremity, would give in at once and cry quarter, but, instead of that, he all of a sudden drew a large pistol from his belt and presented it at the face of the tall sailor, who was so overcome at this (not expecting it) that he let the short sailor pick up his sword and begin again. Then, the chopping recommenced, and a variety of fancy chops were administered on both sides; such as chops dealt with the left hand, and under the leg, and over the right shoulder, and over the left; and when the short sailor made a vigorous cut at the tall sailor's legs, which would have shaved them clean off if it had taken effect, the tall sailor jumped over the short sailor's sword, wherefore to balance the matter, and make it all fair, the tall sailor administered the same cut, and the short sailor jumped over *his* sword. After this, there was a good deal of dodging about, the hitching up of the inexpressibles in the absence of braces, and then the short sailor (who was the moral character evidently, for he always had the best of it) made a violent demonstration and closed in with the tall sailor, who, after a few unavailing struggles, went down, and expired in great torture as the short sailor put his foot upon his breast, and bored a hole in him through and through.

'"That'll be a double *encore* if you take care, boys," said Mr Crummles. "You had better get your wind now and change your clothes . . ."

'"What do you think of that, sir?" inquired Mr Crummles.

'"Very good, indeed – capital," answered Nicholas.

'"You won't see such boys as those very often, I think," said Mr Crummles.

'Nicholas assented – observing, that if they were a little better match –

'"Match!" cried Mr Crummles.

'"I mean if they were a little more of a size," said Nicholas, explaining himself.

'"Size!" repeated Mr Crummles; "why it's the essence of the combat that there should be a foot or two between them. How are you to get up the sympathies of the audience in a legitimate manner, if there isn't a little man contending against a big one – unless there's at least five to one, and we haven't hands enough for that business in our company . . ."

'"It's the main point," said Mr Crummles.'

There are three points from the above extract of particular interest. One is the mention of the type of swords used, 'short broad-swords with basket hilts which are commonly used at our minor theatres'. This could be taken as a 'dig' at the minor theatres for always using the same weapons no matter what the period of the play. Secondly, it is noteworthy to read of the use of surprise when the tall sailor disarms the shorter one, who thereupon thrusts a pistol in the face of the tall sailor, and is able to retrieve his sword and get on with it again. Something of a cliché these days, no doubt, but it was

'The Country Manager Rehearses a Combat' etching by Phiz of the Crummles Family for Nicholas Nickleby by Charles Dickens.

obviously what the audience of the time loved. Thirdly, it seems that the best 'fancy chops' were saved to nearly the end (building up the audience's fervour!), prior to the short sailor making a particularly violent demonstration for the dénouement. Crummles knew his stuff!

It was often the practice for fight moves and strokes to be handed down – a set sequence already known by the actors saved a great deal of time and rehearsal. This was hardly creative theatre, but at least it could be performed (which is probably the reason for its being done) with the maximum confidence and fury, sparks flying in all directions. The audience demanded an exciting combat, and must have shown their displeasure in no uncertain manner if they witnessed anything at all tentative through under-rehearsal. The type of actor-manager who would instruct his company to deliver their lines no nearer than arm's length from him must also have expected his opponent in the combat to be able to perform a well-known routine with competence at the first rehearsal. I wonder whether they were permitted to be as near for their sword-play as their dialogue!

It is recorded in *The Playgoer* of 1903 that Esmé Berringer 'had the honour of taking the chair at Captain Hutton's interesting lecture at the Playgoers Club on Stage Fights'. Until comparatively recently, in the early 1960s, it was the custom in theatres and drama schools for a Fencing Master or 'A Master of Fence' as he was more grandly called, to be employed to teach and stage fights. His knowledge and experience of the theatre and actors was to say the least, in most cases, limited. Alternatively, an actor who had some kind of, even limited, fencing experience would be given the task of doing the 'fight bit' for a little extra money and customarily not even a credit in the programme! Should a proper fencing master be employed, it was the director of the play who more often than not would put the fight into dramatic form, the master only being required to set the strokes and rehearse the moves. In the 1960s, with experts at everything popping up in all branches of the theatre, fight arranging too became a specialist activity, and stage fight directors needed theatrical experience which they effectively combined with some kind of martial art expertise. The younger reader or less experienced stage combat practitioner will appreciate then that there have been changes. They have mostly been for the better, as that ever-wonderful Hollywood swashbuckling look gave way to one of greater reality to suit the times – but also I would suggest, a little for the worse.

When I started in the theatre in the 1960s, as far as I was aware, with a few notable exceptions (and I think of Bernard Hepton, John Greenwood, Ian McKay and Laurence Payne as well as the excellent Paddy Crean), those actors arranging fight scenes were not very good sport fencers. Certainly, the sport fencing masters had little knowledge or experience in the theatre. Catch 22! In the major drama schools such as The Royal Academy of Dramatic Art and The Central School of Speech and Drama, splendid fencing instructors such as Professor Betrand and Bill Harmer-Brown were teaching as well as Professor Froeschlen and the redoubtable instructress who went to Paris as Sybil Drew and returned as Madame Perigal! Understandably, theatre was not their profession, so what they were teaching to young trainee actors was, from all accounts, the modern sport and not techniques and an approach which was directly applicable to the theatre. I remember at The Central School, where I was a student, at the end of our fencing course we were shown four positions with the rapier and dagger which we were informed would be suitable for the stage, but that was it! As with everything else in the theatre at that time, stage combat became specialised, as a subject in its own right, the new breed of teacher combining a good theatrical background with fencing or martial arts expertise. Thus appeared, for the first time, the modern fight director/arranger. This was better for drama students, who now had specialised tutors of stage combat teaching them, with drama training and experience, rather than sportsmen – people who related fight techniques properly to the theatre and made them integral to character, scene and situation. I don't mean of course to imply by this that never before had fight scenes been arranged creatively from a proper understanding of the play, for who can possibly know, but from research and viewing early silent movies, it would appear that hitherto, spectacle was more the requirement. I remember once when I was a young tutor asking the Registrar at The Central School of Speech and Drama why she thought fencing had always been taught as a drama school subject and without pause for reflection, she replied 'for grace and deportment'. I very much doubt whether anyone today, asked a similar question, would give the same reply.

Still thinking about the 1950s and early 1960s, although obviously there were fight scenes superbly arranged and performed, for example the duel in Olivier's film of *Hamlet*, there were plenty of others which were not. Techniques, if those blade whackings could be called such, looked as if they were derived from children' games of sword-play in the back garden via the movies. A vicious circle. Fight methods of the times had been copied I suspect from watching the old Hollywood swashbucklers and the fights in those must have themselves been derived from theatrical stuff of the day. So here we are again, back at movements from the sport of fencing but unadapted to make them more realistic. One only has to see that look of high line hack and parry which can still be viewed sometimes even today in the theatre and film, from those that know no better, to know that this must have been the case. Those repetitive and uncreative early routines of the Victorian period which I shall come to shortly I'm afraid are round and about and alive and well.

When I was a drama student and had an interest in developing theatre combat, there was no such person as a 'stage fight teacher' to whom one could go to train, because there was at that time no such subject as Stage Combat. Thus, there was no alternative but to develop a system and approach of my own which I imagine is what most people did in the business, if they didn't merely copy from Hollywood. I freely adapted complicated fencing moves and techniques to make them theatrically viable, which could work for unskilled and sometimes unphysical actors, to make them look good. Moves which could be performed easily and with brio which were designed for safety in their execution. From the sport I took those moves which I considered had choreographic appeal and adapted them in a way to be theatrically effective. The intention was that the overall look of the fight should be more convincing than that of those early swashbucklers, whilst maintaining safety to the artists, and provide pictorial and conceptual variety. Thus I hoped to add additional dramatic intensity and excitement.

I remember my good friend and expert stunt co-ordinator Richard Graydon explaining to a new group of young stuntmen during a break in filming 'In the old days, every stuntman was happy as they had in their repertoire, three very effective moves for swordwork. Then, Bill Hobbs came along, added a fourth and made it *complicated*.' Dicky's wry comment probably states the case! What now has happened, however, is that we have some fight practitioners with a modest theatrical background and very moderate fencing experience whose training has been based on the *simplified* systems of theatrical combat. They teach and use such basic methods as the 'be all and end all' without having a solid sports fencing or alternative martial arts base, which in my opinion is a pity. They possess a collection of moves, impressive to the novice but with nothing in support underneath. A glittering bauble but with a hollow centre. Actors, and even would-be arrangers, having learnt stage combat at drama school, can come away thinking how easy and what a lot of fun it all is, but unaware that methods of sports fencing and other sport combat skills with all the wide vocabulary of movements involved, have been very much simplified for their benefit.

A recent editorial in *The Stage* newspaper stated that 'In the course of their working lives – and to broaden their appeal during periods of unemployment – actors pick up the rudiments of many skills. Detached from "real life" by the nature of the calling, they are inclined to forget that what they have acquired is only a veneer to assist an illusion. They are frequently too willing to confuse picking up a few tricks of the trade with the ability actually to ply that trade and every extra skill becomes another line on the C.V. which is an almost mystical symbol in the relentless pursuit of work.' I hope that anyone who thinks that you can pick up stage combat skills in a few sessions will take note. Actor Simon Callow for example states in his book *Being An Actor* that 'There were no classes at the Drama Centre in fencing, dialects, or clog-dancing. They reckoned that if you needed them, you could pick them up in ten minutes. They were right.'

The thinking has clearly moved on, for theatre schools, such as the Drama Centre, now have Stage Combat on the curriculum. To be kind to Mr Callow, it can only be that such a statement as his comes from a lack of understanding about a part of the fight director's job, which is to make the actor *look good*, feel confident and perform skilfully. Sometimes one has the good fortune to work with marvellously physical actors who enjoy what they are doing and that's a wonderful bonus – then, the sky's the limit. Other than that, it's down to the skill of the arranger to devise moves which the actor takes to and can perform easily, for it is only then that he will perform at his best. One must always be on the lookout to change quickly moves and sequences which are not readily being assimilated, for if an actor's left with a routine, part of a routine or even a move with which he feels uncomfortable, he will never perform with real intent and assurance. Simon Callow goes on to state 'Stage fights fill me with particular dread (the one in *As You Like It* was terrifying) mainly because so many actors, once the adrenalin is flowing get the scent of blood in their nostrils and suddenly, you're face to face with a psychopath.'

With proper training, such a 'dread' can be addressed and overcome. I remember the great Austrian actor Klaus Maria Brandauer, when playing Hamlet, saying to a nervous new Laertes with whom he was about to duel, 'you just have to get on with it and forget about potential danger. Start

Sleeves might have been a hindrance to lesser actors but nothing got in the way of this fighting Hamlet. The superb Klaus Maria Brandauer playing the title role in the Borgteater production of Hamlet.

thinking about accidents and you're finished.' Olivier gets it right when he says 'There is a traditional paradox in reference to stage fights "the safer the more dangerous". Most accidents can be attributed to hesitancies and other symptoms of not wishing to hurt your opponent.' That too is my experience. If anyone is going to be hurt, it will be the nervous, hesitant performer and not the actor who is secure, positive and well trained.

To conclude, it wouldn't be right were I not to own up to the fact that I actually directed the wrestling match at The National Theatre which Simon Callow refers to in his book, and I remember that he coped well with everything I asked of him. Furthermore, John Dexter the director of this production said that it was the best *As You Like It* wrestling match he'd ever seen and such praise from John was rare. Personally, however physically unco-ordinated or nervous any actor may be, I am happy to work with and help anyone who is ready to have a go. This was all I expected from two highly respected opera singers whom I remember having to admonish after a particularly lack-lustre dress rehearsal: one of the couple came back with 'Sorry Bill, but you know you've got two queens up here'. Needless to say, they got stuck into the fight at the very next performance and gave it the lift-off that was needed.

2.

Stage & Screen

Whether working in the theatre or in film, I find there is little difference in the actual process of blocking a fight sequence apart from choice of moves, as some look better on screen than others which are too stagy. It's everything else which is completely different. Stage work is rehearsed, the floor marked out, props supplied, the play is teched and opens, all according to a well-tried formula. On the other hand, when filming, one has to be incredibly flexible and prepared always to make changes according to location, set dressing, light and camera positions. Over the years, most directors have shot, without making any alterations, exactly what I have prepared (they can always fiddle and adjust in the editing room afterwards) but as an example of what can go wrong and where cinema differs from the stage, there was a particular fight scene in Richard Lester's *The Three Musketeers* which was to take place on an ice lake, between Michael York and Christopher Lee as hero and villain respectively.

We were to shoot this scene under a hot Spanish sun in the middle of summer, just outside Madrid. There were, as one would expect, not many iced-up lakes to be found in the vicinity and, therefore, the lake was built outside on the open ground in a hollow. If I remember correctly, the surface was a mixture of wax and glycerine which, when watered down, would resemble the real thing, both in appearance and characteristic slippiness. Unable to plan and rehearse the choreography 'in situ', owing to the lake's construction taking place, I prepared with the Spanish stunt doubles and actors on one of the stages at the Madrid Film Studios. Knowing, as I thought, what to expect of the surface and the way it was going to behave, I took this into account and carefully planned falls and slides into the routines between and in conjunction with the sword-play. We experimented with the footwear and generally did everything right, so that on the day of shooting we would be ready. We even had especially made up for us an area on the floor, covered in exactly the correct mixture of wax and glycerine on which we would be performing. We tested it, put water down on it, ran on it, fought on it, slid and fell down as planned. As far as we were concerned, there was nothing which hadn't been anticipated and everything was fine.

Revolutionary realism. Young protagonists in heavy and realistic jerkins (no lightweight shirts) performed with full acted aggression.

Franco Zeffirelli's legendary production of Romeo and Juliet *at The Old Vic Theatre, London. Left to right: Alec McCowen (Mercutio), John Stride (Romeo) and Tom Kempinski (Tybalt).*

Fine that is, until the day of the shoot. That was when the Special Effects Department watered down the surface of the 'lake' using fire hoses from a nearby engine, until our fighting surface was awash with water and the effect of this was to make it so slippery that it was pretty well-nigh impossible to stand on it, let alone fight. Catastrophe! The poor actors, try as they did, were unable to keep upright for any length of time to do their prepared routines, although heroically endeavouring to get within striking range. Our planned falls and slides and almost the entire routine became impossible to perform. All that preparation and choreography had been rendered useless in one grand gesture with the hoses. Hardly a thing went right and though the actors were magnificent in attempting to keep their routine together, fate was not on their or my side. As soon as they managed to rise to their feet, over they went again. They fell, they slid, they crawled, sometimes separately and sometimes together, like a pair of synchronised swimmers. I was grateful to them both for managing to keep together even a few sections of the old routine and fascinated by the new moves which emerged! Special Effects Department 10 – actors and fight arranger 0. Well, somehow, something usable came together, which was I imagine due to some pretty nifty work in John Victor Smith's editing room. From this tale of woe, it will be obvious that there is an enormous difference between doing combats for stage and screen. It is of course this very kind of challenge which makes filming exciting and, at times, nerve-wracking.

It has been said that staged fights can be enhanced in the cinema by effects, the use of doubles and altering camera speed, the implication being (usually from those with little cinema experience) that this makes the task easier than in the theatre. The latter is certainly not true but, to some degree, the former is. Arranging for movies is an altogether more complex affair, because the fight director is dealing with far more than the simple arrangement of a routine and training of the actors. The fact that it is more complex is exactly what provides the additional, if different, satisfaction. Of course, the judicious use of doubles for actors and occasionally speeding up the action with the camera can help the end result, but I've sat through many rushes or 'dailies' as they are known in the States, and the performance level, if anything, has to be even greater than in the theatre, as the camera sees any imperfection. An underpar performance will be shown for what it is, unaimed moves will be seen, and any stagy action shockingly revealed. There have been occasions when I have been very relieved that viewing theatre lights have to be out whilst showing rushes. It may also be of interest, for the inexperienced to note, that you can only ever so slightly speed up the action of fighting, just taking the edge off, without producing a Mickey Mouse/ Keystone Cops look.

As far as the use of doubles is concerned, directors naturally prefer to use the principals, primarily as a shot can be ruined if the face of a double noticeably appears, but also the different way a double moves can be a real give away. Doubles are fundamentally a safeguard for cover as far as I'm concerned. So if for any reason a principal has to stop shooting, work can continue in some way, shape or form. They also stand by as a *performance* safeguard, to lift the level of skill, commitment and drive, when an actor isn't up to it. Even though sometimes the doubles may not need to be used for actual shooting, as was the case for example in the film *Dangerous Liaisons* because of the ability of the actors John Malkovich and Keanu Reeves, nevertheless I always have them well rehearsed and standing-by to cover any eventuality. If, in the event, it turns out that they are needed for shooting – owing to lack of availability, agility or ability of an actor – then money may well have been saved as shooting of the fight scene can continue. Further-more, walk-through rehearsals and camera line-ups can and usually will be undertaken initially by the doubles, thereby saving the actors' energy for the 'take'.

As well as this, a good fight double can be extremely helpful to his principal in ways other than performing for him, such as standing in for rehearsals, assisting teaching a routine and assessing hazards in advance of trouble. As an example of the latter, imagine an actor being required to fight whilst making his way down an incline which is both rocky and slippery, the banks leading down to a river perhaps. In such a situation it will most

The deadly elegance of duelling with the small-sword in 1780. John Malkovich as Vicomte de Valmont duels with Keanu Reeves as Chevalier Danceny for the honour of young Cecile in Stephen Frears' award-winning film of Dangerous Liaisons. © 1988 Warner Bros. Inc.

probably be the actor's action double who will work out in advance where necessary hand and foot holds need to be made. It has to be said that losing a star during filming may not only be a human, but also a financial, disaster. A stunt double or the fight arranger will look out for hazards, such as an overhanging branch or a hole in the ground, and make them safe before the actor bangs into the former or disappears down the latter. Then, there is the situation in which a long shot is required, in which the combatants are so far away as to be mere specks on the horizon or down on the ground, when they couldn't be distinguished from a couple of warring ants. When this is the case, why use the principals?

So I say hooray for those unsung heroes who make those actors who are unphysical or under-rehearsed look good on the screen. I don't mean to imply that all actors are necessarily less physical than the average stunt double; on the contrary, I have worked with some fine athletic actors, and remember with gratitude the splendid work for example of Terence Bayler playing Macduff in Polanski's film of *Macbeth*. He began at the start of rehearsals and pre-shoot training finding not some little difficulty in keeping a good balance, but by the time we shot the final fight, due to lots of hard work, he ended up doing the fight far better than his stunt double. The thing is, that an actor can *act through* the fight, something a double may not be trained to do, and the *acting* of the fight and those particular moments within it is vital. Of course though, more often than the other way round, in terms of physicality it is the fighting double who is the superior combatant and, after all, he is being paid to commit with full fury. Stars are often credited with having performed all their own action, but those who know better seldom let on they know. Alternatively, there are those actors who are keen but without the physical ability to back it up; and they need protecting from themselves. Better this though every time than the disinclined or lazy. As in all walks of life, so too in film and theatre combat, you get the good and bad, committed and uncommitted. There are those fight arrangers who can barely fence or move, actors who would be better off as stuntmen and stuntmen who would be better off as actors and raconteurs.

I believe that the very nature of filming places greater stress on the actors, and additional demands not made in the theatre. There is, ultimately, only one short period to 'get it right' and then, once it is 'in the can', that's it, for better or worse. No second chances. No 'Oh we'll rehearse again before tomorrow night's show and do it better.' All is done. Of course the director and editor will work on putting the scene together afterwards, and music and sound effects will usually be added, but the performance is over and cannot be improved. The editor can only juggle about with the bits of film he's got. Nearly always, therefore, the performance level needed in filming I find is greater than in the theatre. It's like a hundred metre dash – the entire team, after what may have been weeks or days of preparation, is finally ready to go and when 'action' is at last called, the actors, stunt doubles and everyone involved, *have* to get at it with real energy and commitment. Apart from achieving a good result, anything less, with the entire film crew watching, inevitably can mean loss of face for, after all, film units from the camera operator to the loader, from props to Special Effects have at one time or another seen it all. It will take some super special performance to win their approval. Richard Graydon tells a nice story of a Prop man moving the wrong props into the wrong position on the set and balled out by the Director shouting at him 'Joe, haven't you read the damned script.' 'Yes' came the ready reply 'Bloody awful.' There are of course though those actors to whom loss of face seems singularly unimportant.

For example a particular Robin Hood, I remember, was about to perform the famous fight on the log with Little John at their first meeting. The log straddled the banks either side of fairly fast running water, but the only danger was about 9–13m (30–40ft) away, where the river turned into a waterfall. Every safety precaution had been taken for the actors. We had

The start of the combat – fully armed with swords, axe and shield. Weapons striking against fully armoured bodies, instead of blade simply meeting blade, give a thudding reality to the combat, in keeping with the reality, in the time it was made, of the film.

Terence Bayler as Macduff and Jon Finch as Macbeth (left).

safety lines, they had spiked shoes, and even a hidden platform running alongside the log to widen it, so that no one could slip off when not planned to do so. Safety lines ran across the water from side to side and stuntmen and water experts in their wet suits were standing by up to their waists in the water. Despite all this, as I stood on the log, I heard the star approaching the scene behind me, saw him huddled up in coats, tentatively walking onto the log and muttering 'I hate this, I hate this.' He didn't give me a lot of confidence either. The problem of his lack of commitment was solved only by the usual close-ups of the actor doing short bits of the stave routine, and mostly covered by two excellent doubles in long shot – and the verve and fighting intention of a splendid Little John.

In the theatre, a fight has to be repeated night after night safely and securely with nothing ever changing or allowed to change. There are no outside factors to be considered – no running water, no light changes, no new positions, no dodgy uneven ground, etc., no horses charging through fighting knights in armour who can't see through their visors. Nothing to affect what has been rehearsed and no situation changes, such as new set dressing unexpectedly appearing. Everything is set and remains set. Therein lies a great part of the security. The only interruption I can recall to a planned stage fight was hardly dangerous or challenging. When setting the 'fight over barriers' in a production of *The White Devil* at The Royal National Theatre during the Olivier regime, I was working with two slightly greying 'savage warriors' who faced each other, either side of one of the barriers. In their right hand they held large knives and the left gripped a chain ring which held them together. In such a linked situation, they fought with furious brutality until, just prior to climax, they were stopped in their tracks by the ringing voice of that splendid actor Edward Petherbridge, calling out 'Aren't they a bit old to be fighting over that necklace dear.' The concentration level when rehearsing and performing fights is absolute – mostly!

In filming all kinds of outside elements can affect the performance and have to be coped with. For example, soggy wet feet, working in mud and rain, freezing cold hands on an early winter morning, high heel boots which have to be worn when fighting on cobble stones (as in the duel in *Cyrano de Bergerac*), sheep which won't do what's required of them or that dog which keeps yapping around the actors' feet when they are trying to perform savage combat. I could go on, but apart from everything else that has to be contended with, those involved know that this is their one and only chance to 'put on a good show' and this very factor increases the pressure on them. The stage fight needs to be equally as well rehearsed and performed, but nevertheless, the action doesn't need to be lifted up that extra notch, which is what is needed by the camera, showing as it does every flaw – someone not aiming at their opponent, a blow not connecting, a reaction out of time, etc. In the final duel between Rochefort and D'Artagnan in Richard Lester's *Three Musketeers*, as the two enter the convent fighting, there can be seen a cut from hero to villain which strikes the doorway too high above the head to be real. Probably this wouldn't be noticed on stage, but the camera sees it, and it's there for ever more on screen. As I have previously said, to do the same routine in the safe and friendly environment of a theatre set is not at all the same, as performing it on the edge of a cliff in the pouring rain when one has more than simply the routine to concern oneself with.

It is essential when working on a film to liaise with all departments regarding the action, for often the finished result will very much have been a team effort involving the Art Department, Costume Department, Armoury and Props and not forgetting, in certain situations, Special Effects, Animal and Horse Departments. As an arranger, miss a trick and you may have mucked up a shoot, which doesn't go down at all well with the First Assistant, Director and Producer. Mistakes can mean delays and to quote the old adage, 'time is money'. Imagine for example a move in which a character is thrown up against a rock and this has not been discussed

William Hobbs rehearsing Richard Chamberlain and Frank Finlay for The Return of the Musketeers.

between the Arranger and the Art Department with the set being constructed indoors on a studio stage. On the day of shooting, or perhaps a day or so before, the Arranger discovers that the rock provided by the designer is unstable, as he hasn't been told that it is to be used in the action and it has been made of polystyrene. What now? If whacked against, it is going to move about violently in shot and it is too late to do anything about it. What can be done? The alternatives are to change the moves, thereby changing the actor's routine at the last minute (not a good idea) or requesting the Art Department to supply a new and stable rock (more cost). Neither at such a late stage will go down well, but it will go down even less well if the problem is not resolved, and time is lost on the day of shooting by a combatant hurling himself into a lightweight piece of the set which wobbles about when bashed against, thus ruining the shot.

I recall arriving early in the morning for the first day's shooting of the Ridley Scott film *The Duellists* and, because the budget was extremely tight, we had the very minimum number of swords to work with. Because of this, I had been rehearsing the day before with the actors back at the hotel, some forty minutes drive away, with the very swords which would be required for use in shooting the opening fight scene. Unfortunately I discovered that I had not brought them with me in the car but left them behind in the hotel. Horrified, with about half an hour to go before we were to walk through the duel for the camera, I sent the car back to the hotel for them, which to my enormous relief returned in the nick of time, together with the weapons. Had we started on time, there would have been no weapons and to fight without swords would I think have presented something of a problem. Note to self – the Arranger must not only not miss a trick but also not forget the swords!

Finally, think about creating a battle scene involving 500 fighting men. This could never happen on stage but if memory serves me accurately, that was the number we used in the battle for the film of *Cyrano de Bergerac* and it took enormous preparation and organisation to achieve the impression of mass chaos which was finally depicted. Maybe we didn't have the 'cast of thousands' as in the old Hollywood epics such as *Ben Hur* but 500 was ample to cope with, all having to fight at once. We actually used a mixture of Hungarian stuntmen, as we were shooting in Hungary, young actors who had been auditioned and selected for their physicality and members of the real Hungarian military. The latter group I think enjoyed their escape from harsher routines into the world of film fantasy. Certainly, they entered into the spirt of mock battle and pretend deaths with remarkable gusto. Ironic really to train, as we did, the military to *die* well. They screamed, they shouted and went down with panache, vying for Oscar-winning deaths. Some indeed rather overacted!

The battle was prepared and rehearsed in a large field, marked out into areas where tents and trees would be, and with a ditch dug of the correct length and shape to resemble the barricades which would be encountered on the actual set. Soldiers and battlers were allocated areas in which they would do their stuff and to where they would move. There were individual and group routines which were worked out, and the sequences for the leading characters were all planned in meticulous detail. Well, perhaps not all actually, for Christian 'died' heroically in an *unorchestrated* fashion, hacking away against a mass of enemy spears, as the Spanish stormed the barricades and held his ground, even to death. The action mostly concentrated on Cyrano's story within the battle and I recall one particular point when it was necessary to time absolutely accurately the fighting of two separate groups of soldiers, Spanish army and French cadets, to finish at precisely the right moment to allow Cyrano and De Guiche to meet fleetingly, eye to eye, together in the midst of all the carry-on, as smoke, gung-ho fighters and shooting were happening all around. No easy task. One wrong or mistimed move and the entire sequence (or maybe one should say 'floored fighters') fell down like a pack of cards. With all this mayhem going on, the climax was the arrival, bursting through the now destroyed barricades, of the Spanish horse soldiers to round up the defeated French. A lot of

Bloody and savage. No early Hollywood stuff here! Long and very heavy military sabres were used for Ridley Scott's Cannes prize-winner.

The Duellists. *Director Ridley Scott. Harvey Keitel as Feraud (left) and Keith Carradine as D'Hubert. Photo: Paramount Pictures.*

'Then as I end the refrain, thrust home.' The final duel to verse as Cyrano invents a ballade in Jean-Paul Rappeaneau's film of Cyrano de Bergerac.

Gerard Depardieu as Cyrano and Philippe Volter as Valvert.

stuff to go wrong and fortunately nothing did, apart from minor injuries to a couple of stunt horsemen whilst undertaking falls.

Looking back over my early battle check list (see opposite) I am reminded of the enormous preparation which took place in all departments, and which incorporated the skills of so many fine and talented people, from top to bottom. There was the brilliant and visionary director Jean-Paul Rappeaneau whose planning of every shot in advance was done in the most minute detail, his First Assistant, the remarkable Thierry Chabert, known in the business as 'The Prince' who carried out his mammoth task always with his stylish walking cane in hand, and out of a team of wonderful French talents it would be remiss of me were I not to single out for special praise the splendid Michel Carliez who doubled Gerard Depardieu in a great proportion of the fight and battle scenes. There is no doubt that without his talent, commitment and ability, we could not have achieved the result we did. And finally, not to be forgotten are those ever-willing Hungarian stuntmen and my team from the Hungarian army. An amalgamation of talent and commitment. That's filming.

Against insurmountable odds, Christian dies a heroic death fighting against Spanish spears during the final battle of Jean-Paul Rappeaneau's film Cyrano de Bergerac.

Battle check list

- We need lots of replacement barrels for cadets to reinforce fortifications.
- Lightweight cart to fall.
- Check with Jean-Paul. De we actually see barrels fall or cut back later to wider opening in fortifications?
- Men, tents on fire?
- Check ladders for climbing fortifications.
- Flatten earth for Christian to stand on top of fortifications.
- Stunt and Military Training. Rifle Drill.
- Check wooden spikes sticking out of fortifications, for safety.
- When does Michel, Gerard's stunt double return?
- Cyrano's halberd. We need lightweights. Check repeats.
- Rehearsal space needed (field) for battle rehearsal – marked out exactly and with true representation of fortification area – trench, etc.
- When is Gerard free to rehearse first duel?
- Retractable spikes – 2 required. One to screw into to soldier for F.G.
- Who fights next to Cyrano? De Guiche?

- Lightweight barrels required. Real ones will cause injury.
- When will all the weaponry arrive and be ready for rehearsal?
- Pikes too long for horsemen – check if same ones as viewed.
- Muskets don't load!!
- Some dummies needed.
- Doubles for De Guiche and Le Bret. Select if required.
- Something required to cover the end of spikes as men climb over.
- Take pikemen through (over the top) first.
- For Christian – some opponents with swords and some with pikes, or all with pikes?
- *Impossible* to actually fight with the long pikes.
- Do we want different sections of the fortifications to cave in separately – small at first and then growing larger?
- When will the horse rehearsals with gunfire be?
- Do we need to see Le Bret and De Guiche fighting?
- Perhaps make spike heads detachable.
- See the balsa spikes I ordered and check how they break.
- See idea of roping of tree to pull spikes down.
- Ladders not required – as trench too small.
- Cart idea – reinforcing barricade – gunpowder, blows up and fire.
- Carbon and Cyrano passing the flag.
- Tent – men inside – blood – collapse.
- See long spikes pushing fortifications over – could then break.
- Decide areas for staging of set pieces of action.
- Dummies required. Important so we can re-use stuntmen.
- Will Christian die in shot? A. No.
- Give De Guiche 'orders' he can be calling out to his men.
- Check surrounding at end with the horsemen and 'Cyrano running everywhere'.
- The Army will mostly be firing guns and the stunts and young actors fighting. Use army for background stuff.
- Exact position of tents – check.

Small beginnings!

The plans on pages 39–41 show the original conception upon which an approach to the scene of Cyrano's Fight Against 100 Men was based. The notion was an attempt to get away from the unrealistic look, when Bruce Lee or John Wayne fought against the masses, by confining Cyrano to fighting only small groups of opponents at any given moment, in a variety of different settings.

From Jean-Paul Rappeneau's film Cyrano de Bergerac.

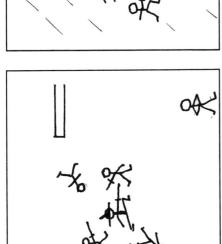

1. Cyrano jumps from wall onto group of waiting men. Ligniere the poet watches.

2. Cyrano fights the group. Ligniere watches in amazement.

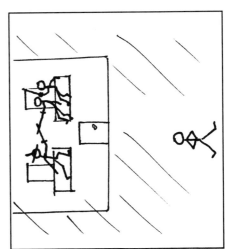

3. Fog wipes out scene

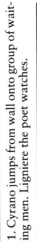

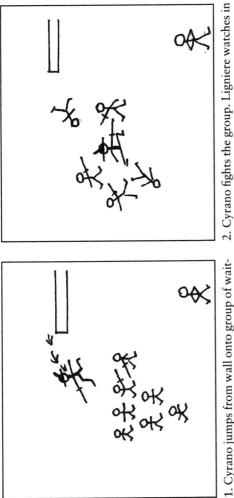

4. Fog clears. No sign of Cyrano. Where is Cyrano?

5. Assassins run through streets – followed by Ligniere – looking for Cyrano.

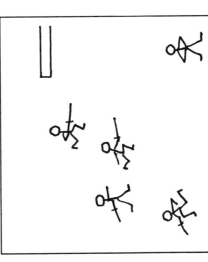

6. Ligniere turns and sees Cyrano through fog, fighting on balcony. Perhaps see Cyrano come down rope as fog again obliterates the scene.

9. Ligniere hears fighting – turns around and sees through the fog Cyrano fighting on roof or scaffold – men fall.

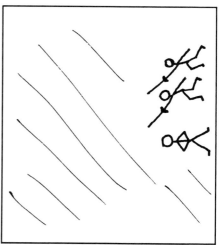

12. Now sees assassin thrown through window into barn – Cyrano leaps in after. More fighting in barn. Maybe young lovers caught surprised. Cyrano exits through window and lost in fog.

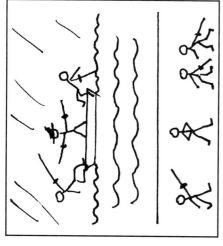

8. Fog clears. Ligniere sees Cyrano fighting in boat – knocking assailants into the water. Fog obliterates scene from Ligniere and men's view.

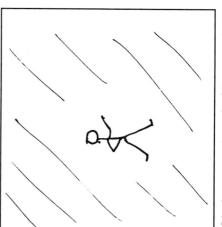

11. Ligniere staggering – looking around sees nothing – again hears fighting and sound of breaking glass.

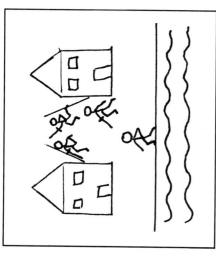

7. Ligniere (drunk) staggers down to waterside, followed by some of assassin group. Where is Cyrano? Again disappeared.

10. Fog obliterates. Ligniere and men move in direction of fighting.

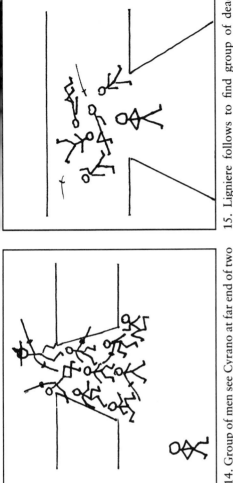

15. Ligniere follows to find group of dead/wounded men. But no Cyrano.

14. Group of men see Cyrano at far end of two converging walls and give chase BUT as only one can get through far end at a time, Cyrano easily despatches, one by one.

18. . . . disappears into fog, sheathing rapier as he goes.

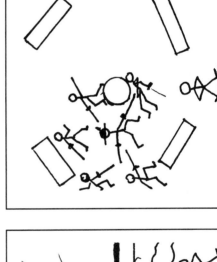

13. As fog clears, Ligniere sees assassins on some kind of pedestal/statue/scaffold with flambeaus. Cyrano on bridge above – pushes whole lot over (somehow!) cut supporting ropes. Fog wipes scene.

17. Maybe final piece of joyous Cyrano fighting in square. Cyrano finishes his task – some run away as Cyrano moves for moment with Ligniere, and . . .

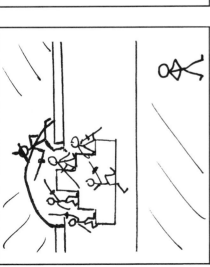

16. Ligniere walks and then sees through fog Cyrano push away a plank (forming bridge between two platforms over water) and those following fall into water.

3.

Analysis & Construction

Quite obviously, it is essential before beginning work on any fight arrangement – no matter how slight the skirmish – to know the play and to understand the function of the characters. No two people move or react in the same way, and the personality of each of the characters will determine the way they fight, and govern everything they do during the fight sequence. People who behave in a distinctly individual way throughout a play or film cannot and must not merge in personality when fighting. Broadly speaking, if careful consideration is given to a man's physique, intellect and personality, an idea will be formed of the probable way he will move and fight. Clearly, to have two or three minutes of unceasing sword-whacking will be pretty meaningless. It only conveys to an audience 'this is where these two men fight', and that is all. It tells us nothing about the characters and will add little to the development of the play. Even in a well-known piece, where the outcome of the fight is common knowledge, the audience should entertain an occasional doubt as to whether or not the author's known intentions are going to be fulfilled. It is essential that the fight tells a story and develops the drama.

Initial discussions with the director, set designer and costume designer are essential before planning anything. Particular note should be paid to both costume and scenic designs for they can both aid and also hamper the action. It may be possible to influence the designs at an early stage, but once the making is underway, the combat will 'as sure as eggs are eggs' be moulded to fit in with *them*, and not the other way around. Set and costume alterations can prove expensive – fight moves not.

Having decided upon an approach to the fight, which arises out of a firm grasp of the play and its characters, the next task is to start devising a rough shape. Occasionally an author will give a shape to you. If well written as a scene, it can be a great help if the moments of action, as in *Hamlet*, are interspersed with dialogue and business. The dramatist tells the story for you – or rather he indicates very firmly how he wants 'his' fight to be – so the dramatic shape is already defined. The peaks are there, and it is the task of

Costumes and the light-weight cup-hilted rapier, with modern épée blades, by their lightness facilitate movement. A wild attack in the final duel.

Peter O'Toole (Hamlet) and Derek Jacobi (Laertes) in Laurence Olivier's National Theatre opening production of Hamlet. *Photo: Angus McBean.*

the arranger to work out how he leads up to them. The majority of authors, however, give little or no help in this way but the authors I hate are those who with a little second-hand knowledge tell you in their writing what moves to use, 'Navarre does a double doublez, parries and ripostes at incredible speed, finishing in a pirouette and a hand spring'. Try to perform that, and you'd be in a real twist.

So, a shape has to be created. By this I mean dividing a fight up into phases of action, pauses, incidents, character moments, business and even additional dialogue (with the author's approval), depending on how it is felt it should run. Of course, there are those fights which are intended to appear shapeless in effect, but even these, the apparently formless, need the same careful planning as any other type or style. Paramount is maintaining truthfulness to the text and telling the story honestly, which of course should not limit imagination – ever.

No one, of course, tries to knock the hell out of someone else non-stop, when their lives are at stake, apart from perhaps the sort of drunken, mind-blown assault in which thought has gone out of the window. Every type of situation is different, but in a certain type of fight where one mistake may mean death, the combatants may possibly display caution and therefore there will be pauses in the action. The excitement of a dead-stop after a piece of really fast fighting, with neither character daring to move a muscle, can be tremendous, like two rattlesnakes poised for attack. So, for all sorts of reasons, there will be action and pause or moments between, breaking up the monotony of relentless action. This in itself can be thought of as a crude shape. To be thoroughly simplistic, there might be a long piece of action, followed by a short pause, a single movement or stroke followed by a longer pause, but this is not a creative way to embark on arranging a fight scene. I think one should merely be conscious of such possibilities – not plan in fits and starts. The fight must grow organically from one sequence to the next. Pauses anyway are never there for their own sake. The fight is a whole, to be acted through from start to finish. Non-stop action or moments between sequences are equally as false if not *acted*. Nothing, unless maybe when 'pyrotechnics' are required in a piece of spectacle, should be done for effect. Rather, everything, move and movement must be choreographed into the fight because it has a place and feels right for character and situation. Nowadays this is probably stating the obvious but it's always worth a reminder and reaffirmation. In almost every piece of work I do, I find that I'm editing, chucking out bad ideas and bringing in others which are more appropriate, as I go along. Sometimes, I'm sure it's not easy for the actors to work, but at the end of the day one just knows when one's achieved the right result, which is truthful, exciting and inventive.

It is impossible to make rules, for all depends on the text and the story to be told. Some fights are over in a flash – they are not really fights at all, maybe just beatings up or killings and so quick that not a lot of analysis or

The reality and muddy effect of Shakespearian battle: no stylised formations.

Coriolanus, *Royal Shakespeare Company, Stratford-upon-Avon. The central figure, Ian Hogg in the title role.*

construction is needed. A quick stab or two, gurgle and *finito*. Mostly, though, there will be variations, brought about either by outside influence (other people on stage, scenery, props, etc.) or by the main characters themselves. Incidents will disrupt the pattern of organised combat. Whatever the emotions, they involve changes, which provide variety, and variety and invention are the essential ingredients of all fights.

Finally, although the director will usually give the arranger a free hand in conducting the fight episode, this will nevertheless have to be in accordance with the agreed concept, so it is important to attend rehearsals of the complete play to enable the fight to grow truly out of the whole, and not to be a mini-spectacle divorced from the rest of the piece.

CUNNINGHAM/GUTHRIE FIGHT.

From the film *Rob Roy*, United Artists.

It is important the director understands the intentions behind the blocking. The fight should tell a story.

To be read in conjunction with numbers on ground plan moves.

Guthrie salutes. Cunningham salutes.

1. Guthrie beats the gun and attacks before Cunningham is ready at the end of Cunningham's salute.
   (Moment C's anger at this)

2. Cunningham responds by driving Guthrie back. This sequence should set up Cunningham's skill and Guthrie unable to cope with it. We see Cunningham immediately showing who's boss. I imagine the crowd have not seen anything like this before in this arena. Cunningham's slice to Guthrie's chest at the end of this short burst is blocked as an immediate reply to Guthrie's previous 'out of order' attack. It is 'tit for tat' – only far more vicious (Guthrie furious at being shown up) and . . .

3. Guthrie makes wild attack in response, but Cunningham avoids this adeptly. Immediately he nearly runs onto Cunningham's point. He knows he has and Cunningham knows he has. See Guthrie sensing danger. Guthrie holds back his natural desire to attack the popinjay who is making a fool of him but cannot contain the need to attack which is exactly what Cunningham wants and

4. Guthrie attacks several times driving Cunningham back but in so doing is wounded four times at great speed. We see Cunningham's deadly ability and there is SHOCK. No more so than for Guthrie when at the end of the four hits he sees the blood where he has been hit on each occasion. BIG MOMENT. Guthrie totally dishonoured in front of everyone watching. He has been taken apart.

5. Now Cunningham corners Guthrie and in a way torments and plays with him. He could finish him off but chooses not to. Guthrie progressively desperate and

6. Now out of control he makes wild and desperate attempts for Cunningham's blade. There is little left.

7. Cunningham struts, assessing the poor quality of the opposition and decides to tighten the screw one notch tighter. He is enjoying the discomfiture of his opponent. He drives Guthrie back, who gets too close and makes the slice for 'Gutted' (as hard or as light as is needed). He struts away, a man merely doing a job. The fight so far has been leading to this moment. Again he could kill or finish the man, but chooses to make him suffer and continue. After this Guthrie's spirit is broken. He becomes more out of control as he is personally becoming more shamed in front of the onlookers and his boss.

8. Cunningham winds up into a final drive back, which is noticeable for the ease with which he performs it – almost walking. Guthrie has now pretty well completely gone and Cunningham very casual about the task. The 'bull' is almost ready for 'the kill' but even now Cunningham holds back, faces Guthrie and waits for him to attack – *sadistic*.

9. Guthrie *moment*, summoning up will power for a final effort. He makes big swipe – frustrated and demoralised. Cunningham has no problems – sidesteps and flicks Guthrie hard on the back. Guthrie falls.

10. Guthrie from floor makes last half-hearted effort but gets put down by Cunningham. Punch drunk by it all and disgraced, he grabs for Cunningham who forces him to the floor in an arm lock and brings the point of his sword to Guthrie's throat.

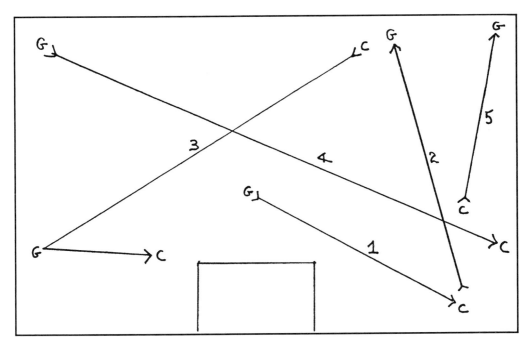

<u>A</u>

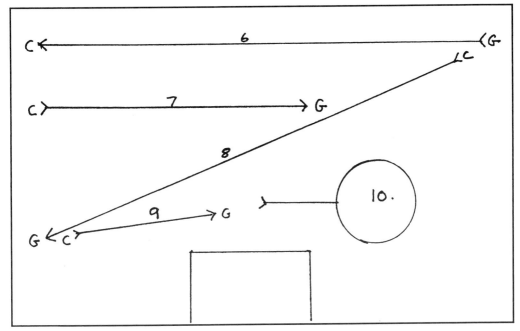

<u>B</u>

ROB ROY/CUNNINGHAM – FINAL SEQUENCE.

Story Notes as per Diagram Numbers.

1. The speed and ferocity of Cunningham's initial attack is astounding and Rob knows now, he is facing a lethal and technically superior swordsman. Even Rob's greater size and strength is obviously going to be of no avail, as he is driven back in retreat, stunned by Cunningham's sudden and dangerous onslaught. It is clear that the point is superior to the edge.

2. Rob tries to attack but it is no use. Cunningham moves faster and even has the audacity to show in advance what he is about to do – quickly making his first *strike*, and delicately wounding Rob on the chest. It is clear to Rob, Cunningham and those watching, that there is no contest and it is only a matter of time.

3. Taking advantage of Rob's wound, Cunningham drives Rob back again and we have a pause – eyeball to eyeball with neither man giving ground.

4, 5, 6. Cunningham attacks, fast and dangerously, with three feints, around the left side of Rob and then the right, stopping Rob whichever way he turns – each time Cunningham is there first, obviously faster and now growing in confidence and enjoying the situation. He is winding up for strike two and it is clear that he is dealing with Rob as easily as he earlier dealt with Guthrie. He could finish Rob at anytime but *chooses* not to – a cat playing with a mouse, until at the end of section 6 he *strikes* again, this time for Rob's shoulder. He could easily follow up and finish the task but doesn't, rather simply moving away, leaving Rob to suffer the indignity and pain of what has taken place. This is the awfulness. Just that Cunningham *waits* and *enjoys* Rob's suffering, knowing that Rob has to continue for his honour. He knows that unlike Guthrie, Rob will never go down or give up.

7. Summoning up all his strength, both physical and of will, slowly Rob moves toward Cunningham for what is a final full blooded effort, ignoring the pain in his chest, side and shoulder. The long sequence which follows is all Rob on the attack with Cunningham avoiding this way and that. It is a long, superhuman effort which leaves Rob exhausted, having given all he knows how. Cunningham sees his opponent has 'shot his bolt' and . . .

8. speedily deceives Rob's attempted bind of the blade, forcing him back and then . . .

9. launches into another series of attacks, moving all around Rob, this way and that, like a 'willo'the wisp' which ends in a final reverse *strike* to Rob's right arm. Rob has now been twice wounded on his sword arm. Again Cunningham doesn't follow up but

10. prefers to casually walk Rob back. He knows and Rob knows the game is up and it will soon all be over, but still Cunningham chooses only to torment and not finish his man.

11. Cunningham waits, seemingly inviting Rob to attack, which he does and twice Cunningham easily and arrogantly avoids. Rob's two last moves are those of a broken, defeated man. He is mentally and physically drained. Sadistically Cunningham leaves Rob bleeding and moves away, turning back only to wait for Rob to come to him for the *coup de grâce*. There is no other option now and Rob stumbles slowly forward towards Cunningham.

12. When Rob goes to attack, Cunningham casually and simply strikes a blow across the chest and side which sends Rob to the floor where the ending and final reversal will be delivered.

N.B. The overall feeling for Cunningham is that he is a man merely going about a job.

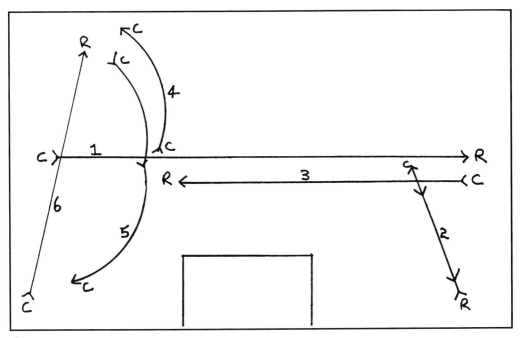

A

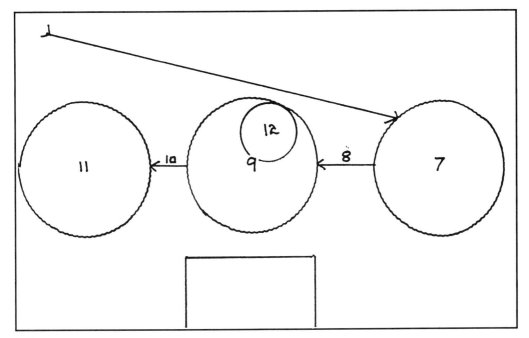

B

4.

Movement & Shapes

I have always been very conscious of the choreographic pictures being presented to an audience throughout the fight. Here I have in mind two distinctly separate things: the actual patterns made by weapons and bodies, and the overall movements of people about the stage.

Dealing, perversely, with the second subject first, it should be obvious that except when two sloggers are hammering away at each other, fighters hard at it will not remain in fixed position. They will move because they have to, either 'controlled' or 'out of control', for numerous different reasons. In attack, or in retreat, they will move, fast or slowly depending upon what is happening; they may move to gain the advantage of height, to induce their opponent to make some error in order to counter-attack, or simply in panic. So too on stage, always dependent on the situation, the characters will move in various ways, and these moves will be planned (according to the ideas of the arranger, actors and director) to grow from an analysis of the text and characters. The object is to let the overall movements evolve without imposing them while at the same time creating a variety of positioning. The good arranger will have a feeling for the emotions of the characters which will lead him to block moves in accordance with the actors' ideas and conception.

Allowing all this, there are then certain technical requirements. It is important to plot moves in such a way (a) as to position them in order to exert their greatest effect on the audience, ensuring that the best are not hidden or viewed from the wrong angle, while at the same time masking any tricks which should not be seen; and (b) to make the most of a variety of positioning, changing this wherever possible in the light of the situation in order to present a change of picture and to maintain the audience's interest.

The reader will notice that in the diagram opposite (the last violent part of a *Hamlet* duel) as great a use of the stage as possible has been made, and a pattern of movement has been created. The on-stage spectators' moves are too involved to relate here, but their diverse movements in, around, between and away from the two protagonists were used to accentuate the sudden

A sequence of blade strokes performed by two combatants – the patterns recorded by the addition of tiny bulbs to the tips of the blades. Variety in the planning of moves, leads to pictorially vibrant pictures and shapes as displayed here. Photo: Chris J. Arthur.

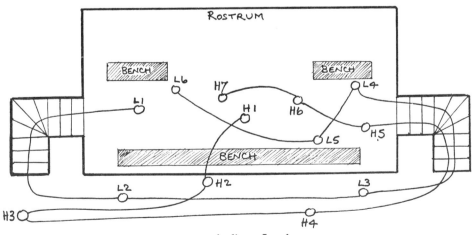

Audience Level

danger of the situation, thus creating visually and emotionally a more powerful climax.

As to the movement of bodies and various strokes of the weapons, they are making patterns all the time. When working on the initial construction, it is worthwhile spending time on ensuring choreographic variety to create pleasing patterns, which consist of *logical* movements – but not flamboyant for their own sake, unless flamboyancy is called for, in which case, they are not for their own sake. Always, the fight intention must be maintained, that is the governing rule. To be side-tracked choreographically into making pretty pictures might have a place in a ballet or perhaps if stylisation or a very particular effect is required, but not otherwise.

To conclude, the audience will lose interest when there is constant repetition of the same moves – unless, of course, the situation is such that a repetitive bludgeoning effect is called for, so pictorial variety is vital.

5.

Fight Orchestration

To discuss a fight in musical terms, and to talk about its rhythms, will probably sound incongruous, and perhaps pretentious. However, possibly because of a vaguely musical background (I own up to having been a leading chorister in a cathedral choir school, more handy at fighting off unwelcome missiles during the sermon than rendering a devotional *Fight the Good Fight*), I have always been conscious that most well-constructed fights have changes of rhythm and are 'orchestrated' in a way not unlike a musical score. For example, a fight may, like a piece of music, start in low key at a slow tempo and gradually gain in momentum and pitch, arriving eventually at the equivalent of a clash of cymbals. This can be followed, perhaps, by a period of uneasy calm shattered occasionally by phrases of 'staccato'; the *rallentando* until the next crescendo, and so on until the final climax. Without this orchestration, or shape, a fight will not only run the risk of being excessively dull, but will probably emerge as an unorganised mess.

How often has one seen a stage fight which contains virtually the same rhythm and feeling throughout the entire sequence, and lacks any change or variety of mood. To extend the musical analogy further, it is as though the actors are performing a fight equivalent to *Chopsticks* over and over again with relentless monotony. The restriction of every combat to the same kind of tempo, without variety or punctuation, will have a soporific effect, and will ultimately – albeit unconsciously – lose the audience's interest. There is no dogma to define the positioning for changes of mood and rhythm; all that is necessary is an awareness of the need for such variations from time to time, as the situation requires. In my experience, it is only when one is in actual rehearsal that rhythmic changes of feeling are easily effected, and the need for such changes perceived. They can be planned in advance, but this is limiting to creative ideas and the organic growth of the episode. Cinema of course creates its shape not only by the work of the arranger in rehearsal and during shooting, but most importantly, afterwards in the editing room, when many favourite bits can end up on the floor.

I am of course talking generally when I say that various extraneous sounds and noises are an additional necessity to the fight, as well as changes of mood and atmosphere, and are as vital as are percussive moments and tonal variation to a symphony or concerto. Obviously the majority of stage skirmishes cannot be enacted truthfully and effectively if the only sound to be heard is the faint clash of weapons wielded by silent combatants. Murmurs and shouts from the onlookers as they react to what is going on, screams, bells – in fact, any noises that derive solely from the fight alone – will not detract from the action, but will support and heighten it. The fighters too will usually need to share in this 'percussion', for without sound of some kind the effect can be like a silent film of the Keystone Cops – all dash and go, with no piano in the pit. In films the sound of steel on steel often has to be dubbed on after shooting, to heighten the effect and to create excitement. Occasionally when I have asked an actor for a shout at a particular moment he has questioned the validity of such a direction, not feeling the need for such an expression. If, however, he had seen the film *The Seven Samurai*, or fenced to four-all, when everything depends on the final hit, he would understand how a vocal explosion arising from the pit of the stomach comes readily and naturally to a combatant launching an attack after a period of tension when lives are at stake.

When energy is held back, and out of desperation is suddenly released, vocalisation is a natural extension of the attacking move. Until the actor is able to execute the moves of a fight confidently as if second nature and the acting performance takes over he will of course feel that shouts are alien. This is to be expected, but it is vital that at some stage of rehearsal the sequence is acted through vocally as well as just physically, because the vocal side of things can be easily missed and its very real significance lost. I am of course referring to the majority of situations, for there will always be exceptions which require different handling.

To sum up, and to clarify this rather difficult analogy, one need only to listen to a tiny snatch of a well-known musical piece to get the idea. H.C. Colles says, 'It was a favourite device of Beethoven suddenly, when one expected familiar things, to open up a new vista of harmony and shake off the fetters of convention. Since the coda is the place where one begins to foresee the end, he particularly loves to give something unforeseen there.' Colles goes on to talk about the way Beethoven uses an element of surprise in the finale of the Sonata in C Minor (op. 10 No. 1), where just before the end he checks the flow to introduce the second subject which gets slower and slower in the remote key of D flat major. He gradually lulls his hearers to rest, and then, with a sweeping arpeggio, picks up the thread of his discourse and makes a rapid end – so rich and varied are the sudden transitions of Beethoven's codas that one might fill a volume in examining them.

So too with fights – dark and light passages, punctuation – in fact, contrasts, change and variety.

6.

The Element of Surprise

An alternative chapter heading would be 'The Quest for the Unobvious', for in dealing with combats, inevitably much the same situation is often repeated under various guises in different plays. To find the right approach for this or that particular scene may require a real search for an idea which will bring the fight in question uniquely to life. Take for example the commonplace hero/villain situation – D'Artagnan v. Rochefort, Robin Hood v. Guy of Gisbourne or even Macbeth v. Macduff, all climactic fights coming at the end of the story. Different weapons will probably be used, according to the historical period in which each play is set, which helps – as does the involvement of very different characters – to produce varied treatment. Nonetheless, the danger remains of a single approach to certain fights, owing to the basic similarity of the situations.

With the richness of background of a play like *Macbeth* there really is no excuse for the fight not to grow truly out of the story, but consider the case where the author has given little character information upon which to build the fight. Then you have a cardboard situation, and the only way this can be brought to life is by searching for ideas and possibilities which can lift the scene into reality and surprise the audience, by the use of the unexpected. Life will be brought to the fight by ideas — movements alone, however well performed, are really insufficient. To repeat well-tried moves and even ideas in different plays with a fundamentally similar situation is the easy way out, particularly when a piece may only demand a light-hearted skirmish. This can never be the creative art of fight direction.

We, the audience, have our interest held by the characters. What they are suffering, what's going on in their head during the conflict, what they hope to do or achieve, how they outwit, outmanoeuvre or perhaps cover with bravura their true feelings. The list and possibilities are endless, but always relating to the situation. The concern is with characterisation and to deal with a scene properly according to the story. Blocking out the right moves is important, of course, but only a part of the job. The discovery and presentation of little personality quirks and eccentricities, the moments of

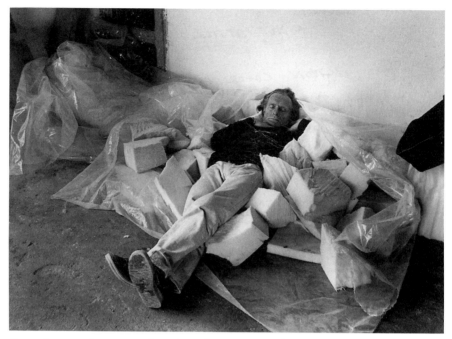

Stunt Arranger's own explanation of picture: 'To the untutored eye, this appears to be a man asleep. Not at all. This Action Co-ordinator has closed his eyes in order to concentrate more fully on the next scenario. He has assumed the "recumbent position" – essential to deep meditation – and advocated for many centuries by the mystics of Tibet, Mongolia and the Upper Himalayas.'

Richard Graydon outside studio whilst filming in Tunisia.

unexpected invention, the element of surprise, the enaction of the unusual, not just for its own sake but because such a thing *could* happen, even though it be not explicit in the text – all these give the real texture to a fight scene. The incorporation of the unobvious, even though this must always be dependent upon the truth of the scene, will enrich the fight and give it life, particularly in those cases where the author has given a stock situation without a great deal of information for the fight director to go on. I well remember the movie script which was sent to me to read, instructing that the last set piece encounter between hero and villain was to be 'the greatest fight in motion picture history'. Oh really? Just like that?!

Like any choreographer, the director of a combat scene will have a repertoire of moves which he will employ, dependent on the situation. These moves he will employ in different permutations, and perhaps with flair and variety, but still in the end it is not these, but the IDEAS behind them which are limitless. It is perfectly feasible, even within a set structure, to shed new light on familiar situations, while remaining faithful to the text. It is these ideas incorporated within a fight structure, just as much as the skill and exciting performance of the participants, that will enhance the combat and give it dramatic shape. The two requirements go hand in hand. The fast attacks of the fighters and the ring of steel should it be a sword-fight are all very well, but can be boring unless supported by originally thought-out happenings that could only be displayed by particular combatants in a particular situation. Of course, it is not only ideas involving the fighters themselves which matter. The discretionary use of other characters on stage, lighting effects, props, sound effects and music can all enhance, clarify and invigorate a situation when used imaginatively.

So then, to sum up, changing focus by the use of ideas which are in keeping with the text, inventing through the characters, the situation and the times in which the play is set are very important facets of an approach by which one can bring a fight scene to life, and give it meaning and dramatic structure.

7.

Safety Precautions & Method of Rehearsing

*H*aving planned the fight in rough and given it overall shape and structure, it is imperative throughout rehearsals to employ certain safety procedures which ensure to the best of human endeavour the safety of the actors and all involved. Of course there are those difficult personalities one has to work with who, in my heart of hearts, I wouldn't mind receiving their comeuppance but all have to be looked after, the good and the not so good. In retrospect I even care now about the welfare of that impossibly young arrogant actor-would be film star, who would insist on giving notes on how it should be done to his internationally famous film star 'opponent' in a recent period movie. I forgive too the European minor star who claimed serious leg injury before we were about to shoot a big fight sequence. The entire unit agreed he was feigning as he hobbled around the set on crutches. Was it fear of what was to come? 'My double will do it', the blond god presumptously informed me but maybe it was the insurance money he might be able to claim from the company that was behind it. I shall never know, but it must be mentioned that the 'injury' was caused when walking from a fall due to the 'uneven surface' of the studio floor. Very strange.

Then, I remember with great affection the number one drinking star who was in the habit of throwing swords around the set while the film crew ducked behind cameras and sound trolleys when his stunt opponent forgot a move, although it was quite clear that his lack of ability to remember moves with a hangover was the likely cause of the mistakes. There was the leading man in a West End production who couldn't accept that his character should ever not be on top when fighting, even though he would have been even more loved by an audience who already loved him, had his character won through *in spite* of enormous odds. I inwardly cursed them all at the time, but every actor has to be looked after when fighting no matter how difficult and I remember those above with some wry humour for the challenges they presented. I could go on, but you get the idea, and over the years I have also

Reach and stretch out! The look of intention in the attack. A good distance between the two, and Mercutio bends down low.

Hans Henrik Voetmann and Per Moller Nielsen as Mercutio and Tybalt in the Odense Teater production of Romeo and Juliet, *Denmark, 1978.*

been privileged to work with some marvellously physical, intelligent and listening actors, so it's always swings and roundabouts.

Anyway . . . no matter how appealing certain business or movements may be, if they present any possible risk they must be revised or if necessary rejected, for it is essential that the actors feel confident in the moves they are given, and in their ability to carry them out. It is paradoxical that a fundamentally safe move can be performed dangerously, and a dangerous move executed safely.

Provided that a well-rehearsed drill and precision routine are faithfully maintained, safety can be achieved, even at full speed. Moves and positions must be carefully worked out and rehearsed, for discipline and control are the very basis upon which a safe fight depends. Rehearsal time is another all-important factor contributing to the safety and success of any fight. It is impossible to create anything worthwhile with insufficient rehearsal, and attempts to do so are likely either to prove dangerous, or to look amateurish, or both. Very few actors are trained in a martial art, and therefore there may sometimes be a certain reluctance or even fear in the case of a nervous actor, when called upon to participate in a fight. With this in mind, it is essential that confidence is built up gradually, and nothing rushed.

The first stage of rehearsing a sword-fight should be concerned with the synchronisation of footwork with the various movements of attack and defence. For example, when one person takes a movement forward the other must take a corresponding move backward, and vice versa, so that at all times (except when purposely out of distance or in close), the same amount of space between the two is maintained. It should then follow that provided the actors start at a safe distance, it will be preserved throughout an exchange. Accidents can occur for many reasons, including getting too close, and when this happens movements are inclined to get muddled and blades to miss, thereby forcing the actors into unrehearsed and inaccurate movements. One fundamental safety precaution I have always employed, although it may not be apparent to an audience, is for the actors to work out of distance. That is to say, when one makes an attack the opponent's body is out of reach, but the blades are just able to make contact. This not only means that the point of a blade is short of the target but it forces the attacker to stretch right out in order to make blade-contact, thereby creating far more dynamic movements.

Another basic safety measure to employ in the planning of strokes is to avoid any movement which goes across the face. An unlucky blow taken on the hand may be painful, but a similarly misguided blow in the region of the face or head could be much more serious.

Probably the most important aid to achieving safety is the very simple matter of communication – talking – letting your partner or partners know what you are about to rehearse in advance, who's going to start an attack or routine, what move you are picking up from and at what speed you intend to rehearse (let's hope it's the same as your partner's!).

From the very beginning it will be possible to work to a definite, well-defined rhythm. The establishment of such a rhythm is of tremendous importance, for no matter how fast the fight eventually becomes, it will always be firmly supported by an inbuilt feeling of timing. Actors in a fight are like acrobats performing a feat; timing and rhythm are essential. Each actor's movements cannot be thought of as individual, but must merge together to resemble an incredibly well-oiled machine, where the different cogs work together in unison.

Most actors prefer to have the entire fight set as quickly as possible, so that they know the work that lies ahead of them. In filming, keeping ahead of the game is essential. A major sequence involving a lot of people and moves should be plotted and rehearsed as much in advance of shooting as possible. Apart from anything else, should the leading actor (and it often is) be involved in a major fight as in *Cyrano* or *Hamlet*, he is likely to be called for shooting most days of the schedule and therefore be unavailable to rehearse. In such a situation and in order to be ready on time, I always try and plan these sequences with the actors involved well ahead and prior to main shooting commencing. I can recall twice at least when there was a gap of as much as two months between blocking and shooting, but that doesn't matter providing the fight is kept warm.

It is a good idea to start rehearsing a phase at a time, working on a new phase as the actors grow confident with the last. The fight should be rehearsed every day until such time as it can be done right through without stopping. At this point originally set positions and movements should be checked – though, of course, a constant watch should be kept throughout. The fight should not be speeded up too soon, or left too late; usually actors will speed up of their own accord as the moves become familiar. It is, however, potentially disastrous to speed up before a movement is seen to be repeatedly executed in a safe fashion. What then is a safe fashion?

Cinema fights at times have different requirements demanding different solutions, but as a simple example for the stage, attacks should be made lightly, and the actors should learn to pull a stroke, so that if by accident an attack is not parried, they are able to hold it back. In a cutting stroke the effort should be channelled forward in such a way that the blade as it were ricochets past the opponent once it has met his blade. The real effort then goes past the adversary and is not directed at him, but to an audience the effect is just the same. Strokes, indeed, must never be made in a heavy-handed manner. With sword-play the wearing of fencing masks during rehearsals is of course optional, but I believe it induces a false sense of security. Better by far to rely on discipline, control and technique which, unlike masks, will afford a real security through all performances.

There is a school of thought which believes that it is safer to aim a stroke slightly away from the part of the body one is intending to hit. I strongly disagree with this idea, for I have found that it is far safer for the defender to know *exactly* where the attack is coming. Otherwise the attacker is going to spend all his concentration on making strokes which just miss the target, leaving the defender to guess where these misses will come, and making parries which are likely to miss, resulting in the actors being thrown, and possibly causing accidents. I would stress that my main concern in teaching actors really to aim for the body is to *avoid* accidents, even though it is only when strokes are correctly aimed that intention – and therefore reality – is achieved.

Lastly, it should not be overlooked that certain types of actors can be a danger both to themselves and to others – one such is the type who will throw himself into a fight more than is necessary in an uncontrolled and therefore potentially dangerous manner, selfishly determined that come what may, he will look good. The other, and equally dangerous, man is the actor who through lack of confidence makes tentative moves. The positive and certain performer is always best, provided at the same time he acts with intention, discipline and control.

Safety procedures

1. Never attempt to speed up too soon. Build up the actors' confidence. Take all the time possible at a moderate rhythm. Speeding up a fight should be a gradual process.

2. Always work in good light.

3. At all times wear shoes that won't slip or slide, and if you are in costume ensure that shoes have rubber soles.

4. In sword-play concentrate on never getting too close through un-disciplined footwork except when choreographed to do so.

5. Check that all weapon handles are covered with some non-slip material, preferably leather. A sword hilt of bare metal held in a hot, sticky hand is likely to slip and go out of control. Resin for the hands and feet is an added safeguard.

6. Check that the floor is not slippery – non-slip wax, Coca-Cola left to dry and resin powder can all be tried.

7. If possible for sword-work, wear gloves – preferably made of soft chamois leather.

8. Sweep the stage before performance, and give particular attention to removing debris – tacks and screws, etc. – which could prove hazardous.

9. Limber up and rehearse the fight before every performance. This should be done as per performance although not flat out but not merely marked through casually.

10. Never change to different weapons without proper rehearsal. The difference in weight or balance can be a potential danger.

A warning note

Extract from *The Sketch*, 19 August 1896. Re: The Tragedy at the Novelty Theatre:

'Both ancient and modern records can show many a stage mishap, though not often of so serious a character as that which has just occurred. Upon the night of the first production of H.J. Byron's powerful drama *Michael Strogoff* at the Adelphi, 15 March 1881, Mr Charles Warner, in the title role, bearing dis-patches to the Russian Grand Duke, was set upon by Ivan Ogareff, the villain of the piece, played by Mr James Fernandez, and a duel with daggers ensued, in the excitement of which Mr Warner was badly wounded in the hand. But, with admirable pluck, he kept the injured hand behind him, and, though sick and faint from the pain and loss of blood, struggled on till the curtain fell. Only the other day, too, Mr Gordon Craig, playing Macduff, "laid on" with such an excess of zeal that the unfortunate Macbeth suffered somewhat severely about the hand; but not so badly as the unlucky Macduff who lost a couple of fingers in his stage fight with the Macbeth of the great Macready.

'Barry Sullivan once attacked Richard the Third with such vigour that his opponent's sword was dashed from his hand, and they were within an ace of a bad accident; and Mr William Terriss has had at least one unpleasant experience of stage duels. Even more remarkable, in its way, was an incident which occurred in Stockholm early in the sixteenth century. The actor who played the part of Longinus in *The Mystery of the Passion*, and had to pierce Christ on the Cross, was so transported with the spirit of the action that he actually killed the other actor. The King, who was present, was so angry that he leaped on the stage and cut off the head of Longinus; and, finally the people, who had been pleased with the actor's zeal, were so infuriated with the King that they turned upon him and slew him – a veritable tragedy of tragedies.

'In an amateur performance of *Romeo and Juliet*, at the Cathedral Schools, Manchester on 31 March 1891, Tybalt, making a lunge past Romeo, unhappily passed his sword through the body of the youth, with, of course, fatal results.

'Many years ago an Italian artist named Dombardi, who was playing in *Antigone*, had to turn his sword from his father's breast to his own, and in the excitement of the moment plunged it into his body with fatal results. Once in a Chinese Theatre two actors fought a stage duel in earnest from love of the same woman, one being killed before the audience; but cases such as this of deliberate murder are rare. Only a few years ago Mr Barton McGuckin, singing in *Rienzi* at Liverpool, had a narrow escape, one of the crowd approaching him with upraised daggers losing his footing, and falling forward, the dagger passing through Mr McGuckin's arm, and slightly penetrating his breast.'

Nasty, and bearing the possibility of such incidents in mind, when filming I always check when we're shooting a fight that a nurse has been called to be in attendance – just in case! If one is on location, seemingly away from civilisation in some foreign country, then I also find out how far it would be to travel to the nearest hospital in the event of an accident and if far, request that an ambulance is standing by a short distance from the set. Normally all this will have been arranged by the Assistant Directors, but it's right to check. It is best of course that ambulance or nurse is not prominently featured, like vultures waiting for their prey, which understandably can be off putting to the actor of a nervous disposition. This reminds me of a skirmish involving about ten actors in the film of *Cyrano de Bergerac*. I was standing watching the action, aware that the nurse was not around, to discover that she was at the bottom of the hill, chatting with some stuntmen.

Not only was this glamorous creature not about, but there was also no sign of the ambulance which had been ordered. I pointed this out to our producer René Cleitman who was standing next to me, and when at the conclusion of the sequence I noted an actor collapsed in a chair with people all around looking at his eye, I just glanced at René, I'm afraid with a probable 'told you so' expression on my face, to which he quickly responded with a twinkle in his eye 'Maybe *because* you asked'!

8.

Sword Strokes, Some Basic Movements & Their Execution

A system for beginners

Before continuing, I should like to restate remarks made at the end of the Introduction, that these moves are included not in order to teach but merely as an example of the care, precision and techniques which have to be achieved. It would be wrong to attempt to learn such skills from a book and the moves are only explained to support training under a qualified tutor.

The reader who has at any time fenced will recognise many of the following movements as similar to those used in the modern sport. However, in almost every instance there are major differences to make them more suitable for the stage from the point of view of effectiveness and safety. It is not possible to cover every stroke and movement within the scope of this book; what follows is intended merely as a basis, and the movements have been chosen with the beginner in mind. While one should remember that every period in history has a different technique according to the weapons used, a straightforward fight could nonetheless be developed using the moves described, and it will depend upon the imagination of the planner as to the effectiveness of the end result.

First of all, some basic safety principles.

1. As mentioned in the previous chapter, work (except when otherwise planned) out of distance, so that the attacker in a full lunge cannot reach the body of the defender, but is near enough to make blade-contact.

2. All cutting strokes are pulled so that no strength is directed at the receiver.

3. As also mentioned previously, no movement ever crosses the face, whether in attack or in defence, even when the combatants are out of distance.

Stance (Fig 1)

This, like everything else, depends on character and situation, and each period of history has a different stance. In general, however, a good balanced position is with the feet fairly far apart and with knees slightly bent. This enables movements forward and backward to be executed with speed, while still maintaining balance. The feet do not need to be in a fencer's strict right-angled position, for we are not concerned with modern fencing, but to be well balanced and nimble-footed is important. It will be found that the most comfortable position for the body in most sword-fighting situations is about three-quarters on to one's opponent.

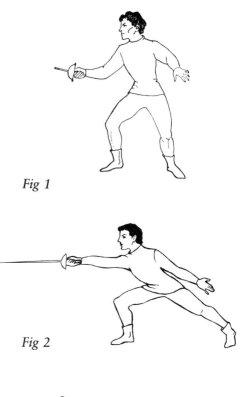

Fig 1

Fig 2

Fig 3

The lunge (Fig 2)

The lunge is used in attack to reach towards your opponent. It is executed by pushing off from the back leg and flexing it from its bent position to a straight one. At the same time the front foot is kicked forward, so that it moves from its original position about 60cm (2ft) (for a man of average height). As in modern fencing, as an aid to balance the left hand should at the same time be dropped down and straightened, with the palm turned up until it is in line with the back leg. In a full lunge position the front knee will be over the front heel and there will be a straight line from the front knee to the back foot which is kept flat, acting as an anchor.

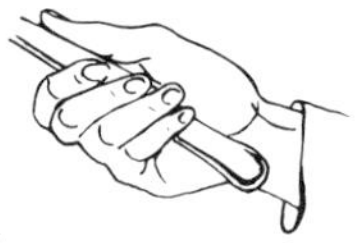

The grip (Figs 3, 4)

Unless the sword is very heavy, a general all-purpose grip is with the thumb lying straight on top of the handle and with the index finger underneath. The handle rests in the second phalanx of the forefinger, and the other three fingers hold the handle in place resting on the side. This position facilitates control, and it is better for the fingers not to be curled around the hilt.

When a heavier weapon is used it may be found necessary for the handle to be fully gripped, by wrapping the hand completely around it.

Fig 4

The basic system of attack and parry

To set down the various methods of attack and defence through the ages would require a book on its own. Assuming that the arranger will do the necessary research into a particular period, the actor's task is to familiarise himself with the deployment of the weapons. Generally speaking, moves of modern fencing (with some notable exceptions, such as the lunge and when used in eighteenth-century small-sword play) are not particularly useful in themselves for the purpose of stage combat. This is not to say that actually being able to fence and move well is not of benefit. It is. I am talking about the actual moves. Modern fencing techniques are for the most part unsafe, certainly when employed within reaching distance of one's partner. This is because the modern sports fencer is trained to *hit*, while the stage fighter is creating an illusion. He only has to *appear* to be out to kill. Also, modern fencing looks on stage exactly what it is, and is therefore useless to depict historical accuracy or a feeling of period. The number of sport fencing scenes in contemporary plays is, to say the least, small. So having put forward what cannot be used, what is the range of options open to the arranger?

Fundamentally, I employ a system of parry and attack, which is adaptable to most periods and situations. It is very easy to assimilate even for absolute novices. The methods are safe in my experience, providing that the principles laid down are strictly observed. Other moves are added to the basic strokes given, to provide greater pictorial variety and elaboration.

Parry positions

For convenience sake, and for use with the symbols given on p. 111, I have given the following parry positions numbers to avoid confusion with their modern fencing counterparts, as they are for the most part not quite the same. We are going to look at five basic cuts and the *blocks* or, as they are called, *parries* to those attacks. There are many more, which vary according to the period, but the following are probably the most useful to start with and serve as examples of the technique required.

The head parry and the two shoulder parries differ from the equivalent fencing positions in that they are pushed further forward, and away from the body, to make for the utmost safety. The two flank parries, which are pure modern fencing positions, will differ too if heavy weapons are employed, as it will be necessary to push these forward and away from the body also, in order to meet the weightier attack that may come with a heavy weapon. If the parry is too near the body the force of a slightly heavier attack which is insufficiently pulled could go through the parry. Of course, when the participants are properly trained this will not apply, as attack will not be made in a heavy-handed fashion.

Parries look far more theatrically effective if they are not passive positions, but really moving into the set position to ward off an oncoming attack. It will be found on certain occasions that if one leans away from the attack when defending the result will be more telling.

The method of making any parry is to meet the top half of the opposing blade nearest the point, with the bottom half of the defending blade nearest to the guard. Here one has fullest command of the opponent's blade, as since it is near the hand, one has more strength, and therefore control of the weapon.

With all parries use the outside edge of the blade to meet the attack, and never the flat. Edge should meet edge.

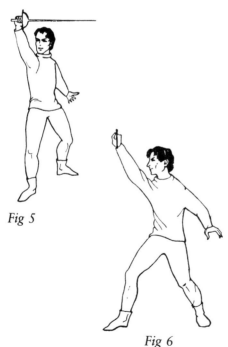

Fig 5

Fig 6

Parry 1 – the head parry (Figs 5, 6)

This parry is made with the blade of the sword absolutely parallel to the ground. The sword is pushed as high as possible away from the head, and at the same time forward from the face. The hand will be held to the front, with the fingernails towards the opponent. The action of lifting the sword to meet the attack should be smooth, with the muscles of the arm and shoulder relaxed. To tense up will slow down any planned reply and tension is never good, which of course applies not only to parries, but generally.

Parry 1a – head parry (Figs 7, 8)

This is an alternative parry to the last and a useful variation. For reasons of safety, however, the novice would be well advised not to use this if the previous parry could be employed equally well. To make the parry, lift the sword arm as before, but on this occasion turn the back of the hand to the opponent, while making the part of the blade nearest the hilt cover the head. The hand will be to the left of the face, and forward from it.

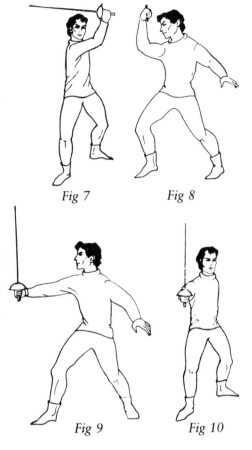

Fig 7   Fig 8

Parry 2 – right shoulder parry (Figs 9, 10)

The blade in this instance is vertical to the floor, and is again pushed forward so that the strong part of the blade is covering the part to be protected. The hand is held just below shoulder-height, with the knuckles three-quarters on to the opponent.

Fig 9   Fig 10

Fig 11   Fig 12

Parry 3 – left shoulder parry (Figs 11, 12)

Exactly the same as for parry 2, only on the left side this time, with the back of the hand three-quarters to the opponent and the palm facing oneself. Particular care needs to be taken with this parry, as on the left-hand side of the body (if right-handed), one has less coverage due to the arm crossing the body and, correspondingly, it needs to be pushed further out to the side and forward.

Parry 4 – right flank parry (Figs 13, 14)

The hand is held waist-high, just a little lower than the elbow, and the palm is turned down towards the floor. The blade is in a diagonal line, so that the strong part of the blade is covering the flank area, and the elbow is about a hand's breadth away from the body.

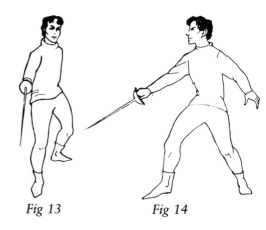

Fig 13   *Fig 14*

Parry 5 – left flank parry (Figs 15, 16)

The palm of the hand is now turned up, and the hand has moved across to the left of the body, again about waist-high. The sword-blade is in a similar diagonal, and the elbow a hand's breadth from the body.

Circular parries

Circular parries mainly used with point weapons can add pictorial variety, but unless the performer is experienced, they should only be made from parry positions 4 and 5. From positions 2 and 3 they could be dangerous, as the opposing point can be swept into the face. Generally they are used with light swords.

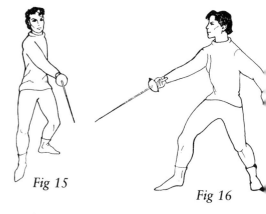

Fig 15

Fig 16

Circular parry from position 4 (Fig 17)

Fig 17

Imagine that one had two duellists, and that B has made a cut to A's right flank, which A has parried by position 4. B then renews the attack by bringing his point over A's blade and lunging again to the knee. A follows B's blade with his own, making his point describe a complete circle anti-clockwise and returning again to position 4. A has now completed the circular parry.

Circular parry from Position 5

Exactly as from position 4, only on the left side from position 5. This time A's point follows B's in a clockwise direction.

Taking control of the opponent's blade (Figs 18a, 18b, 19a, 19b)

This is the action of binding the opponent's blade, and the move can be carried out from each parry position. The effect is to add greater flamboyancy and variety to the blade patterns, but the logic is an attempt to disarm. The method is to parry the attack, then straighten the blade to form a line with the arm, and swing the opponent's blade to the opposite side. As with circular parries, the bind is most effectively employed not on its own but as part of a sequence. The safest positions for the

Fig 18a

Fig 18b

Fig 19a

Fig 19b

beginner to undertake these man-
oeuvres from are the two shoulder
parries, and next the two head parries. Unless an actor is experienced,
binding from the two flank parries
should be avoided, as there is a danger of carrying the opposing point in
front of the face. Binds from low line
parries can furthermore look like the
'art of coarse fighting' unless executed dazzlingly well, and even
then . . . ! I tend nowadays to give
them a wide berth.

It is worth noting in all movements of this kind that the art is to
catch the half of the opponent's
blade nearest the point with the half
of one's own blade nearest the
guard, and a necessary 'cheat' is for
the attacker to keep his arm straight
during the course of the movement,
for if it is bent there is the possibility
of losing blade-contact. Examples of
binds can be seen in Figures 18a and
b, and 19a and b.

Sidestep evasions
(Figs 20, 21, 22, 23)

Avoidances or evasions were in common practice in early rapier play,
and can be theatrically effective as
part of a sequence.

When they were in use, the idea
was to avoid the oncoming attack,
while at the same time stretching out
the sword arm in the direction of the
adversary to run him through. For
our purposes the latter is not at all a
good idea!

Avoidances are executed by one
definite movement of the foot, as
shown in the illustrations, rather
than by a shuffle or jump which will
place one off balance for any following movement. By using these side-
steps it is possible to come straight
back to the basic position again by
merely reversing the action in one
clean movement when the attack has
been avoided.

Fig 20

Fig 21

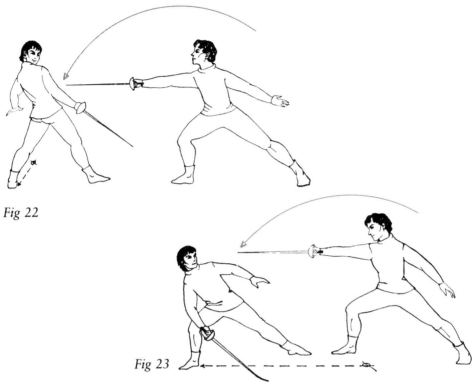

Fig 22

Fig 23

Cuts

We are looking at cuts made to five definite parts of the opponent's body – to the head, to the right and left shoulders, and to the right and left flanks. They will be combined with the lunge in most situations, except when bodies are within distance.

As explained previously, cutting attacks should be made lightly, and strength never used. It is far harder to parry and return the opponent's reply if weight has been put into the original attack. To say that attacks must be made lightly does not of course mean that they need to *appear* half-hearted. It looks unreal to see the attacker's arm not fully extended, and lacking intention. Cuts should always be made with the edge of the blade and never with the flat.

In making any cut it is important that equal time value should be given to the preparation as to the cut. This sets up a rhythm and rhythm is immensely important for safety.

Cut to head (Fig 24)

The preparation for the head cut is made by lowering the sword and swinging the arm either across the chest or behind the back in a circular motion, finally bringing the blade down vertically to meet the parry. At the end of the action the wrist will be flexed, thereby 'pulling' the stroke. The whole action should be smoothly executed.

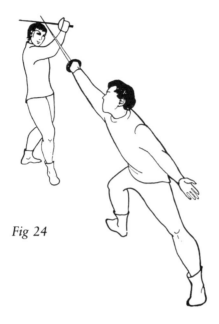

Fig 24

Cuts to shoulder (Figs 25, 26)

The principle here is the same as for the cut to the head, in that there is a smooth preparation of the sword arm (this time bending the arm from the elbow at shoulder-height), while the wrist relaxes back and flexes just before the contact. Try to make the stroke travel parallel to the ground and never diagonally, for one which starts high and ends up low, or vice versa, is potentially unsafe. When aiming at the right shoulder of the 'opponent' the palm will be turned down, and in cutting to the left shoulder the palm will be turned up.

Fig 25

Fig 26

Cuts to flank *(Figs 27, 28)*

Make the cut in the same way, by bending the arm back in preparation, this time at flank-height and flexing the wrist for the hit. Again, as with shoulder cuts, if you are attacking to the right the palm will be turned down, and if to the left, up. The action as with the shoulder cuts should be made to travel horizontally, but starting at the lower height.

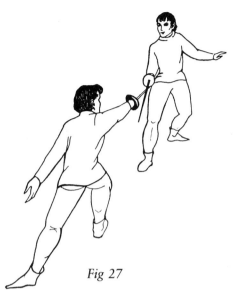

Fig 27

The thrust

Although the manner of the preparation can vary to disguise an often boring move, the thrust with the point is made by a smooth extension of the arm, usually followed by the lunge. For the beginner it should be made only in low line, to be met by the two flank parries, aiming a little above knee-height. Care should be taken that this comes neither higher nor lower. The point must travel absolutely in a straight line from a to b, for nothing is worse for the receiver than a thrust which is waggling about as it moves to the target. To repeat, unless you are experienced never use a thrust above waist-height.

With the arrival of the small-sword in the late seventeenth century, point work predominated, but to limit moves in a play of this period to thrusts in the low line would be unrealistic. The techniques of coping with this problem in order to be able to incorporate moves in high line should be learnt under the guidance of a professional master.

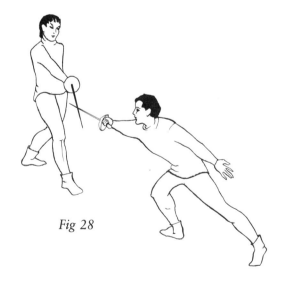

Fig 28

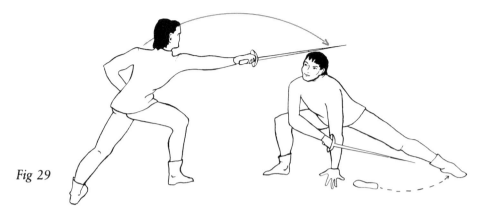

Fig 29

Ducking a cut to right or left shoulder (Fig 29)

The cut to either shoulder will be executed in the manner previously described, but the sword will obviously carry on, as it meets no parry. The important thing is to keep the cut travelling shoulder-height the whole way through the action, running parallel to the floor. If the cut is coming at any sort of angle it is harder to avoid with confidence of safety. When making a cut that is to be ducked prepare the stroke by bending the elbow at shoulder-height and taking the blade behind the shoulder. This will give the opponent a beat – a moment however fast the move is ultimately carried out in which to prepare for his evasion, and the action will have more impetus. There are various means of avoiding, but the simplest is to place the left hand on the floor, while shooting the left leg straight back and tucking the head right down. The head should always be turned away from the direction of the cut, thereby ensuring safety. The only exception is, of course, when one has extremes in height, and a tall man has to duck, while a short man makes the cut. If this is the unfortunate situation, it might well be best to avoid the movement altogether!

Footwork

Excluding turning movements, side-steps and avoidances, characters fighting with swords are going to lunge out and back from a set, safe distance and move forward and backward. The essential requirement is to maintain a safe distance at all times, and this can be achieved provided that footwork is planned to marry with the sword strokes. When a single attack is launched the defender need not move, but if the attacker is to advance the defender in order to keep distance must take a corresponding number of steps back. To summarise, while one is actually trading blows (as against running or moving about) every step and move should be planned, and never allowed to vary.

Body movements with heavy weapons (Figs 30, 31)

In using very heavy weapons (e.g. double-handed swords) it is more effective when there is greater movement of the body. For instance, if in preparation for a cut to the head one only makes the swing from the elbow the true effect of the weight of the sword is lost (Fig 30). The body must be behind the movement (Fig 31), for whether the weapons are in fact heavy or not, if they are big the movements will only look real if the effect of weight is behind them. With large and heavy weapons it will be found necessary to take a larger preparation with every attack (i.e. a swing into the attack). In other words, the supposed weight of the weapons should be 'acted through' with the body.

Fig 30

Fig 31

Four parries for use with rapier and dagger (Figs 32, 33, 34, 35)

These are used to parry a cut to the head, a thrust to the stomach, a cut to the waist on the right, and a cut to the waist on the left. They should all be made with the arms straight and pushed forward and away from the body, maintaining as wide an angle as possible between the blades of the rapier and dagger in which to catch the opponent's blade. It is possible to move from one parry to any of the others without repositioning the blades and hands. For parrying the cut to the head (Fig 32), the palms will be three-quarters on to the opponent. For parrying a thrust to the stomach, the knuckles will be facing the opponent (Fig 33). In parrying a cut to the waist on the right, the palms will be away from the opponent (Fig 34) and towards him on the left side (Fig 35).

Fig 32

Fig 33

Fig 34

Fig 35

9.

Battle Scenes, Mass Fights & Brawls

*T*o generalise about scenes of mass conflict using a lot of people is as wrong as when dealing with duels and fights between individual characters. In a battle scene, little may be known about the characters of most of the combatants, but such a scene is written to make a point, or a variety of story-telling points which have to be observed and shown. Every brawl or battle scene is unique in its character and has its place in developing the drama. The opening brawl in *Romeo and Juliet* is an excellent example, as it possesses a very clear structure. Initially we have the scrap between the servants of the Capulet and Montague households – the lower orders emulating their masters and following the dictates of the ancient vendetta. This leads into Tybalt's set-to with Benvolio, and finally we see the effects of the feud upon the citizens of Verona who themselves become involved in the fray. On top of this and climaxing the whole brawl, even the heads of the families, Capulet and Montague, get to it. Of course it is true that, until the moment when all are caught up in the action, we are actually concerned with separate combats involving named characters. This means that when the scene develops into a general brawl, we already know something about the different factions. This particular brawl has a very clear story line and character of its own. Within such given overall shape, the fight director will also need to create moments of surprise and invention to make the audience sit up and take notice, for if the opening brawl fails to have an effect, it lets down the play which follows. These moments will have to be properly focused and set pieces, which are required to be picked out for the audience, shown clearly. It is all too easy, when too much generalised hurly burly is going on, to miss seeing important planned pieces of action.

We aim in the theatre to reproduce the feeling and mood of mass conflict, to fill our stage box with only, for example, a small corner of a 'battle field' for we are dealing entirely with the creation of an illusion. Allowing that each mass fight scene has its own special and unique quality and, within it,

Three's company: a trio of Captain Reds. Walter Matthau with his two action doubles in the Roman Polanski film Pirates.

characterised moments and incidences, large numbers fighting on stage will require certain general safety techniques. The golden rule as far as I'm concerned is straightforward and simple but absolutely essential – no one should be allocated to, or allowed to stray into, another's space whilst actively engaged in fighting. It only needs an unfocused actor, with or without a weapon, to move out of position and into another's area to cause an accident. Particularly when the combatants are involved with weapon play, they must be given the space to go about their stuff freely and without fear of hindrance.

To be involved in a sequence as a trio, and to suddenly find you're a quartet, can be unsettling to say the least. I recall a moment in Tunisia, filming Roman Polanski's film *Pirates*, a film for which I was asked to direct the fights ten years before it was finally made. Naturally I asked how many fights there would be. 'One', Polanski replied. 'It starts when the film starts and ends when the film ends.' On the deck of a mock galleon Walter Matthau was gamely slashing and parrying a few moves with a couple of Polish stuntmen, when suddenly and completely out of the blue, two or three local Tunisian extras who were simply meant to run past camera during the shot, threw themselves at Mr Matthau in the middle of his rehearsed sequence and pulled him in no uncertain manner down onto the deck. I presume they imagined they were meant to join in the action, get stuck in and give a good show. The crew was as amazed as was I but most of all, it was a surprise to Mr Matthau who had at the time been under the impression that he was winning. No serious problem having been caused, with the Tunisians having been prised away from our chief pirate, the situation had its humour – but on another occasion, such unrehearsed action, however splendid, could well have proved dangerous.

It's always an enormous bonus to have keenness from those involved, and extras are not always the most dedicated bunch (and who can blame them) but, as I mentioned earlier, communication is unquestionably the greatest aid to safety. Next time, I shall have to make an effort to learn Arabic, as obviously those ever helpful extras, willing to give their all and not having been told not to improvise, had thought the idea was to have a go at anyone in sight. Most likely, the local tyrant-in-charge of the supernumeraries had probably said 'get stuck in lads or no pay' and, having no respect for star status, did exactly what they were told. So, it will be readily understood that actors must be given *space* to perform, in most fight situations, with the requisite acted aggression. They should have no fear of inadvertently connecting with an unfortunate third party or alternatively becoming a victim of overzealous and uncontrolled fellow battlers.

Brawls on stage do not necessarily need large numbers of participants to create the illusion of size and when space or budgets dictate that the ensemble is not large, it is perfectly possible, by careful manipulation and use of those involved, to create the effect and feeling of commotion. Gone are the days when it was acceptable for a number of soldiers, apparently engaged in mortal combat, to appear from the wings and battle their way across the stage, only to reappear moments later to make a similar foray in the opposite direction. This just won't do any more – an ill-thought-out relic perhaps of Victorian theatre. How can it suggest a battle of enormous magnitude raging over a considerable area?

So, what are convincing alternatives? Treatments will of course vary but, in general, I believe it is worth considering the use of contrasting pieces of action, personal moments and incidents joined imperceptibly together within the overall battle. The intention being to get away from generalised brawling and concentrating on the specific within the overall scheme, with as much variation as is required for the particular scene. These days by giving less numbers greater use of the playing area, the objective can sometimes be more successfully achieved. Of course, with greater attention devoted to individuals and smaller groups of combatants, the selection of what they actually do will need to be considered with care. In fact, there is a lot to be said for conserving numbers and allowing less people to do more but with greater freedom. The more who are *actively* involved, the greater is the likelihood anyway of movements being hampered and restricted. What then comes across to the audience is fear. Fear of being bumped into and being injured. Hardly a maximum ten in the battle scores. When the effect needs to be wild, and this is minimised through the nervousness of a possible accident, the whole intensity of the action will be lost due to moves being executed in a tentative fashion. In order for acted fury to be given full vent, as said before, it is essential to allow freedom of movement and sufficient performing space, and nothing looks worse in a 'bloody killing field' than half-hearted fearful movements.

Don't give up without a good argument, if the end effect will be better with greater numbers, but the use of less people will of course naturally be welcomed by the financial department. Having said that, there will of course always be those occasions when a play performed in a particularly large space *will* require larger numbers of fighters in a battle scene, but only in proportion to the playing area. Particularly, I have in mind outdoor arenas and large-scale operas performed in venues such as Earls Court in London. If large numbers of combatants should be involved, then it may be worth considering separating those using weaponry from those without and making quite certain that only those with ability and experience are given routines incorporating weapons. They will require more space in which to work and move, and those without weapons usually less. It is also possible when many people are involved to limit the numbers actually fighting to the minimum acceptable, while making greater use of more general movement.

The basic task in preparing any ensemble fight scene is to *time* everything, so that all the pieces of the jigsaw fit. Sensibly this will first be done at walking pace, even in slow motion and perhaps without weapons, with the sequence merely mimed. This will also give the arranger the opportunity to ensure that planned incidents and moments of special importance are given their requisite prominence and are not going to be lost from view. The incidents created will be wholly convincing to the action, not ever spectacle for spectacle's sake, and completely relevant to the situation. The questions which always must be asked are what are the needs of the scene and how can these needs best be met? Finding the answers is the fascination and challenge of creating such a piece. The result will be according to the requirements of the play but imaginatively realised. In most brawl scenes, the positions of the fighters will constantly be changing and the audience's attention directed to various parts of the stage at different moments. It is always necessary to change focus and introduce unexpected events to avoid generalisation and thus monotony. Heaven forbid that a fight scene should be one in which the audience dozes off!

After the initial blocking of moves, when the scene is first run in its entirety, there will inevitably be gaps in the action when an individual or group may have completed a routine, before meeting up with another with whom they are required to perform further action. Sometimes in rehearsal these holes will automatically disappear, as those involved become more familiar with their routines and speed up, but anyway, these gaps may not matter and can even be beneficial, providing that no one *ceases* to *act*. It is only when an actor ceases *acting* in a fight scene, waiting for his next routine, that any hiatus will be apparent to an audience. The rule therefore is keep *acting* and there is *no gap*. Of course if it adds to the effect, those waiting moments between routines can be filled with additional action, but even in reality no one would constantly be fighting unless it's John Wayne. Non-stop action is usually ludicrous and not at all real. Better by far to fill in those moments not with fighting, but with acting, for we the audience are more likely to be involved when we *feel* what those on stage or on the screen are going through.

At the risk of repeating myself, one cannot make rules about creativity but only about techniques and safety procedures. Each individual scrap or fight will be synchronised with everything else happening on the stage or film set and individual combats planned and rehearsed in the usual painstaking manner. When the overall battle or brawl has been put together and run as a scene in its entirety, it will be possible to tell which strokes and moves need to be changed for reasons of safety or effect. The overall plan will usually be worked out in advance, but the detailed work will inevitably develop in the course of rehearsals. Only when the various individual routines have been thoroughly rehearsed separately, and when the actors are fully conversant with moves and positions through doing walk-throughs at moderate pace, will it be possible for the action to be speeded up with safety – and it shouldn't be forgotten that everyone has a different idea of speed. Usually I like to call out the rhythm I want, so that everyone understands and is in accord. Otherwise, there could be actors faster than others getting into the wrong place and producing the danger of an accident. Speeding up needs to be done in stages and the fight or battle not suddenly performed at full lick. This ensures that everyone is together and everything happening at the right time. When the play is in performance, it will be each individual actor's responsibility to ensure continued safety by keeping faithfully to what has been rehearsed and it needs emphasising to all concerned that being out of position by even a small amount, can be dangerous. As with all acting, it is essential that sufficient preparation time is allowed. Without it, precision and safety cannot be expected and spontaneity and danger will be more a reality than an appearance. As a general rule it is true to say that the less time available to rehearse, the shorter and simpler the routine has to be.

Finally, as with any action sequence, it is vital to rehearse before every performance and no true professional would dream of going on stage without having done so. Just as a dancer will limber up before a show, so too must an actor loosen up and revise his routine together with his partner or partners, for timing and rhythms together have constantly to be retuned. No

A woman Cypriot being injured in the brawl which leads from a personal encounter into general escalation, involving the local population.

Derek Jacobi (Cassio), Edward Hardwicke (on the ground) and Petronella Barker the woman Cypriot in the British Home Entertainments film based on the National Theatre Company's production of Othello starring Laurence Olivier.

Storming the castle in John Boorman's Excalibur. *The black smoke from burning car tyres was more a health hazard as it covered face, hair and got into lungs, than return fire from the foe.* © 1981 Orion Pictures Company

performance of a fight can be gone into cold when the scene arrives, for the body, even though trained, will not be capable of following at speed what the mind is telling it to do when another person is involved. The brain, as well as the muscles, needs warming up towards performance pitch. It is not sufficient for one participant to practise his routine in isolation. He will certainly not be performing on his own, and it is necessary for all the parties involved to achieve a physical harmony *together*. The machine needs to be well oiled and not simply the cogs! Failure to warm up properly can be an invitation to disaster and even if it doesn't cause an accident it is likely to produce a poor quality and scrappy performance.

10.

Non-Realistic Encounters

So far, we have been concerned only with fight scenes of a serious and realistic nature. There are, however, other types of combat requiring very different treatment. For example, fights to music, or symbolic and comic fights. Fights, actually, can be pretty comic at times and for the wrong reasons. Some film fights I've watched being shot have been hysterical and have had the entire crew and all except the director and producer laughing when things have gone wrong. We were, I remember, shooting on two Spanish doubles in the end fight of Richard Lester's film *Robin and Marian*, when all watching were strangely aware that something was not quite right. The two noble Spaniards – hulking macho stuntmen – were hacking away at their routine on a hill (long shot) but embarking at the same time surprisingly on their own dialogue whilst fighting. This was in Spanish and to me quite incomprehensible. What was it about? One stuntman in true fashion seemed to be getting more into his role than the other and his voice could be heard ringing over the hill, shouting and screaming at his 'opponent'. The two next started devising their own routine, only this time, the intention was not acted. It was for real. It turned out that the argument was about the moves and who was to do what. The choreographed sequence had gone wrong and they were fighting about who was right about a cut to the leg or shoulder. Anyway it was a damn good set to!

Fights to music

Now, on to a more serious note. Here I am referring to a fight which is really a dance, when the movements of bodies and blades adhere strictly to the rhythm of the music. The Georgian State Dance Company have in their repertoire brilliant sword dances in which the dancers make exciting exchanges in perfect time to a very fast rhythm. Another example of this type of non-realistic fight was to be seen in the renowned Berliner Ensemble production of *Coriolanus*, in which armies came together to the crash of cymbals, parted slowly, and the vanquished then sank to the ground one by one to the beat of the music. The warriors faced each other silently in two lines as the stage revolved, took them halfway round, whereupon to rhythm a further onslaught took place.

As soon as a fight is *set* to music it is almost bound to become unrealistic, even when the actual planning of the moves may be real enough, and not enlarged from life in any way. It is practically an impossibility for the natural speed of the actors' movements not to be held up or speeded up in some way to fit in with predetermined rhythms. This is not to say, as with opera, the fight cannot be performed at natural speed, *against* the rhythm of the music. Sometimes it will be *with* and sometimes *against* – always provided you *finish* when the music finishes and you are not still at it when the great tenor comes on and starts singing. This does not go down well!

In a fight to music, where the rhythm of the music determines the speed at which the fight is set, it is vital to get to know the music from the very beginning in order that the correct rhythms may be assimilated and methodically rehearsed, albeit at a slower tempo for safety. If a fight to music should go wrong by a missed move or beat, it will not be easy in performance to get back to the right place again. When it is not necessary to keep to the beat of the music it will be simpler, as a phase can be begun again or continued without upsetting the total flow of the fight.

Written musical accompaniment cannot be stopped and started at will and is not adjustable, therefore a mistimed move could throw a fight into chaos, as much as a dancer getting out of synch with his steps, if it should cause the action to fall behind the music. Only *live* vamping under the fight can be altered in length to suit a few beats more or a few seconds less. Film fights and action nearly always have music under, but normally it is specially composed to underscore and point the action. The action is not customarily fitted to already written and recorded music.

Comedy in fights

When thinking of amusing and intentionally funny fight scenes seen at the cinema, on television or in the theatre, what is it one may ask that makes them comic? Funny business, funny moves? Usually, not so. Comedy grows out of the situation and character, exactly as does any other kind of fight scene. If, as has been said, a fight scene is simply the drama being expressed and moving on by other means, then a humorous fight, as with any staged combat, is simply serving the intention of the text. When approaching the blocking of a fight which reads amusingly in the script, although the temptation may well be there, what must be avoided at all costs is trying to make the moves themselves funny for effect. Let the truth of the situation always dictate the action. Jacques Charon from the Comédie Française, when directing the Feydeau farce *A Flea in Her Ear* at the National Theatre, was at pains to point out to the company that farce was about ordinary people finding themselves in extraordinary situations. The characters were

As in so many photos of fight scenes, the look here is posed and unanimated. The difficulty must have been keeping still in awkward positions while waiting for the photographer. Legs must certainly have ached after a photographic session!

Martin Harvey as Don Juan defends himself from a double attack in Don Juan's Last Wager, *Prince of Wales Theatre, 1900.*

not in themselves funny. So too with fights, which are extremely real for the characters participating but which may perhaps turn out to be humorous to an audience. Such was the case in Richard Lester's film of George Mac-Donald Fraser's Flashman novel *Royal Flash*, in which the cowardly brag-gart Flashman played by Malcolm McDowell in this *The Prisoner of Zenda* send-up, finds himself confronting the deadly Rudolf Rassendyll played by Alan Bates. Fighting for his very life, our 'hero' is seen to be quite out of his depth and only lucky chance and native cunning save him from a sticky end. The humour comes from Flashman's ineptitude as a fighter which is covered up by swagger, whilst the Alan Bates' character takes pleasure in his discomfiture.

There were many moments of wild comedy but I recall two in particular which, although perhaps over the top, nevertheless were in keeping with the overall style of the picture. The first found Flashman being pushed by Rassendyll backside first into a roaring fire which caused his trousers to catch alight, thereby the heat propelling him forward and his opponent away, like a Challenger rocket. Later there is a moment when a swordless

Flashman espies a pair of crossed swords behind a period shield, mounted on the wall. Delighted, he rushes to draw one and carry on fighting for escape, but discovers to his horror as he pulls at one of the swords that they with the shield are all one ornamental piece and quite useless. Both very visual, over-the-top gags maybe, but the point is that they were not in fact that ridiculous, for such occurrences, in the course of a fight in this particular castle hall set, could have happened. In another Richard Lester film, *The Three Musketeers*, there was a climactic moment with D'Artagnan fighting the villain Rochefort at night.

During a fight walk through, Richard Lester asked Roy Kinnear, playing D'Artagnan's ever-faithful servant Planchet, to uproot a large tree with his bare hands and charge with it to smash Rochefort in the back and save his master. Personally, I thought that our director must be cracking up, for to me the idea seemed both unfunny and rather silly. Certainly it was unreal, for no man could pull a sturdy tree up from the ground using strength alone. Judging from the faces of the crew as I looked around, they were of a similar opinion.

Richard Lester, however, made the ludicrous real, and the idea worked completely, with no one of course questioning the logic. It worked for the reason that for Planchet, at that particular moment, it was a matter of desperate needs requiring desperate measures.

One cannot talk in general terms about comic fights, as the construction and presentation depend entirely, as with all fights, upon the situation and characters of the participants. Whether or not a combat succeeds in being comic depends on the ideas of the arranger and the actors, but ultimately it will be a poor contrivance if not based upon the truth of the scene. When comedy is inherent in the situation, the fight itself will still be planned and played honestly and realistically. Of course, there are some silly moves which are in themselves funny, but only when used in an appropriate situation and context. All is down to judgement. The comedy of these particular moves can be put down to the cliché element and they are in essence no more than fight gags, corny because we have witnessed them countless times before. Charlie Chaplin's boxing match for example in *Gold Rush* if I remember accurately consisted in the main of a series of swings, ducks, kicks to the backside and some shadow boxing and the humour was once again that of a smaller man facing up to an opponent almost double his size. Had Chaplin been smashed to the canvas and blood soaked, it might have been realistic but certainly not humorous. What usually makes the Viola/Aguecheek encounter in Shakespeare's *Twelfth Night* comic is the fact that both are terrified, as is Chaplin in his boxing match, but he covers up the fact and wins by default. Really it is a case of 'there but for the grace of God go I' and the audience's pleasure and enjoyment come because they are not involved – as is the character, fighting against impossible odds, in an impossible situation.

Similarly, one only has to look at the altercation which occurs in the play *The Venetian Twins* by Goldoni. In this, Lelio the fop has been paying court to Beatrice, one of the joint heroines, and fights with Florindo, the friend of the hero Tonino, who acts in the fight on Tonino's behalf (are you with me so far). Lelio wins this encounter by accident rather than skill when Florindo slips over. Tonino himself enters to find his friend fallen on the ground and at the mercy of Lelio, who is just about to deliver the *coup de grâce*. He challenges and fights the now fearful Lelio, whom he disarms. Lelio's immediate relief, displayed by his line 'What counfounded luck! I'm unarmed' speaks volumes, and such a scene, with so clear-cut a situation and with such unlikely opponents, presents the arranger of the fights with a wealth of opportunity for invention.

Expressionism

One would usually decide upon a symbolic stylised approach in the presentation of a fight where it is in keeping with the concept of a particular production, or sometimes to save the day when the actors/singers/dancers are not up to anything else. However, it need not be out of place to use symbolic treatment within a realistic production, and in certain cases it can extend the scope of the combat, setting it completely apart from the rest of the play and giving it a greater dramatic effect. On the other hand, one might decide on a stylised approach for reasons of sheer practicality – for example, when, as I have sometimes experienced, the fight in *Macbeth* is to be performed by a woefully out-of-condition middle-aged actor, past his physical prime, who has difficulty even lifting his sword, let alone using it! The main reason, though, for employing stylisation in the presentation of a fight is to escalate the drama, and to enable the presentation to lift to a more telling effect, by removing it from the precincts of our common experience. The necessity arises in certain instances, when the effect required could not possibly be presented with enough power in normal realistic terms. For a fight to be symbolic the fight impressions or feeling have to be shown, as opposed to an actual set-to.

This can be done in any amount of ways. For example, the whole sequence can be slowed down to lend more poignancy to the action, and to show more clearly the macabre savagery of movements. Alternatively, additional moves can be invented which depict the feeling of combat, outside the actual play.

Certain kinds of stylisation have one great advantage, and that is safety. For instance, in slow motion, or when working out of distance, there is absolutely no reason for accidents. Also there is the additional advantage that body movements can be seen to better effect, and more exciting and adventurous movements achieved.

I still remember after so many years that a very good example of the use of stylisation in fights was the massacre in Peter Shaffer's original stage production of *The Royal Hunt of the Sun* at the Royal National Theatre, choreographed by Claude Chagrin. The treatment was in reality a dance to rhythmic percussion and it conjured up the horrific spectacle of Incas being savagely murdered by Pizarro and his band of Spanish invaders. In theatrical terms (however brilliantly contrived and executed) no amount of realism could have as effectively conveyed the dreadfulness of such a scene.

Stylisation in large conflict scenes can be exciting, but probably best realised in major theatre companies with sufficient time to rehearse, as the demands on the physical and rhythmical abilities of those involved are exacting. There seems nowadays, in the United Kingdom, far more consideration than there ever used to be, given to physical possibilities such as in the wonderful expressionistic theatre of Théâtre de Complicité. Furthermore, many productions now heighten the drama by the use of physicality. This is of course nothing new on the Continent but, until comparatively recently, anathema in England. It is an exciting theatrical development, for at last we are not solely concerned with language. English bodies are finally on the move! Symbolism succeeds where it feeds the imagination of the audience to an extent that realism cannot hope to do.

Sound effects and music backing

Performed in virtual silence, most fights give the effect of watching a silent film without the support of the pianist. Just as he was once needed to add mood and excitement to a film, so do most fight scenes, whether on the stage, in films, or on television, need some kind of auditory aid. It may be only vocal from the actors on stage, or on the other hand it could be a complete musical underscore. It might be alarm bells, the amplified clash of steel, or the taped sounds of a town coming to life at the on-stage skirmish. The range of possible sound effects is exciting, particularly when electronic aids are available. Even on the slenderest budget there are numerous ways to produce stunning sound effects in keeping with the situation, which must, as always, determine all. For example in a battle the harsh sounds of cymbal and drum are in accord with the subject, and setting a fight to sounds of this kind can add to the excitement and enhance the action. Thus music or sound backing can accentuate and heighten the mood, and stimulate the audience's imagination. Its function is to reinforce the overall concept but the sound accompaniment must never become more important than the action which must always be the senior partner, although one must complement the other.

It should perhaps be said finally that sound or music support need not necessarily be confined to large scenes. Individual duels can also be aided by music and sound effects where appropriate.

11.

Historical Accuracy

The further back in time one goes, naturally the less is recorded about fighting methods and weapon usage. It is however an essential part of the arranger's task to give proper attention to the period in which a play is set. The problem is, how far to go in a quest for period accuracy and how much licence to allow oneself in order to achieve excitement whilst following the requirements of the script. Of course, there are no clear-cut answers. Weaponry, and to a degree fashion in dress, dictate the way people move and fight, and down the ages these have undergone considerable change. Duelling itself differed in style and techniques, not only from country to country but also from century to century. For instance, the stance or 'en garde' position was not the same a hundred years ago as its modern sport fencing counterpart. Besides being aware of changes in dress, and familiaris- ing oneself with moves and positions of different periods, it is a good idea also to study personal accessories which could perhaps be useful in the planning of a particular fight.

Of necessity, authenticity will usually play a secondary part to what is theatrically acceptable to a modern audience. Should a fast-moving sequence be required in a particular scene and the correct stance, weaponry and techniques of the period hamper freedom of movement, then it will be necessary to compromise, always providing one is not being completely unfaithful to the times of the play and what was correct. As truthful as possible an *impression* of a particular period's fighting methods, based on careful and accurate research, is the acceptable solution. For example, whilst weapons should appear authentic, they don't need to be the true weight of the period being represented, particularly when this may impede the actors' performance. Having said that, I recall my first view of the costumes designed by Yvonne Blake and the swords I was asked to consider using in Richard Lester's *Three* and *Four Musketeer* films. Although looking magni- ficent, the costumes seemed to me very heavy and baggy to be fighting in, so much so in fact that the body line of the fighters would be lost in action, thus detracting from the final presentation. How wrong I was, for the end result

Scene from Miss in Her Teens *by David Garrick with Elizabeth Hippisley, David Garrick, Hannah Prichard and Henry Woodward, Theatre Royal, Covent Garden, 1747.*

John Henderson, William Smith and Elizabeth Young in The Law of Lombardy *by Robert Jephson, Theatre Royal, Drury Lane, 1779.*

The tongue-in-cheek reality of The Three Musketeers. *Oliver Reed recovers from a kick to the crotch, while Michael York moves in to the rescue! Heavy weapons true to the period, together with truthful costuming by Yvonne Blake, help to get away from the early look of blade-to-blade swashbuckling.*

The Three Musketeers, *director Richard Lester.*

turned out to be the complete reverse. Those bulky, heavy costumes actually helped to give a truth to the fighting and a proper period feel, which got away I believe from earlier, lightweight swashbuckling versions of the story. The fact that they were not so easy to fight in, was a very important factor in achieving that period feel to the action.

Likewise with the rapiers. In a quest for authenticity, I was shown some very long-bladed swords which were correctly in period but impossible to wield with any credibility. We then made the decision to shorten them slightly but not so much as to make them lightweight. They would still not be that easy for the actors to use, as would have been those light cup hilt rapiers with thin épée blades most commonly employed in stage and screen. There would be no way that the performers would be allowed to fight with that speedy lightweight neatness associated with early Hollywood swash-bucklers. So I believe that both the costumes and the weaponry helped to produce an authenticity to the action which was more honest to the period. One must assume, I think, that fighters in whatever historical period must have used weaponry which they were capable of wielding to effect, otherwise there would have been little point in employing their use. It follows, therefore, that if an actor is equipped with an historically authentic weapon which is unusable, he will look somewhat silly flailing around with it. This will lend a speculative quality to the combat, but it may not be quite what the dramatist had in mind when he wrote the piece!

For authenticity of movement and what can or cannot be done, we only have to look at the Elizabethan rapier to see that theatrical adaptation from reality, as was the case in the *Musketeer* films, is at times a necessity, although as mentioned above, our adaptation then was very slight in order to maintain period accuracy. The long sword of this period was not for parrying with or warding off attacks since it was too heavy. For this purpose, the left hand or *main-gauche* dagger was employed. However, when it comes to the final result, a staged fight of this period will be severely limited choreographically, if this accuracy is religiously adhered to. All one is left with for the most part will be thrusts and avoidances with little variety of sword attacks and parries. Usually I find that being entirely truthful (as much as one can be, for the further back one goes in time the less is known) to a particular period will result in a dull and unconvincing fight. Speed of movement often equals excitement, but it is possible to achieve tension and a different kind of excitement in times or situations which require it, without dependency on fast exchanges. A more measured combat, as for example in the Middle Ages when weapons and apparel were altogether heavier and more cumbersome than in later years, can have a macabre savagery which is in itself effective. This is not to say of course that the actual throwing of blows would not have been fast and furious in any period. It would have been dependent upon the weight of the weaponry and the ability and strength of those wielding them. It has frequently been said to me that 'of course, it's easier in film as you can speed up the camera' which will give the effect of speedier action but it may be surprising to note that in the Richard Donner film *Ladyhawke*, the speed of the actors' action in the main combat at the end was actually slowed down by the camera, just a notch, in order to achieve a heavier, more savage quality.

Since little is recorded about very early methods of attack and defence, the best preparation is to study early paintings and prints of the period concerned. Small details will be discovered which should give the end product something of the feeling and flavour of the times. For research purposes, prints, woodcuts and armouries are the greatest aid, and it is wise to seek them out, because even if they cannot offer a complete guide as to how movements were at all times executed, they will provide a valuable basic source of knowledge, giving some idea of how the weapons were held, as well as positions of the body, thus indicating how they might be used. Books

Nina Bouciacault as Peter, Hilda Trevelyan as Wendy and Gerald Du Maurier as Hook in Peter Pan, *Duke of York's Theatre, 1904.*

of the period being researched, as far back as one can get them, it goes without saying are especially helpful. It should always be remembered however when viewing pictures that many show the ornate swords of noblemen and princes. The weapon of the common man and soldier would have been markedly cruder. Nothing changes, and the sword to a large extent was a symbol of status! Also, account must be taken of the artist's often heroic pictorial impression, particularly of war scenes and battle.

Finally, a word about stage armour. Victorian theatre used the real thing on stage and this could be seen in London as late as 1930 in the children's play *Where the Rainbow Ends.* Later, papier-mâché was used for helmets and then entire suits of armour were made of felt and papier-mâché. The lightness achieved must surely have been an enormous relief to the actors wearing them, but there is still something to be said for the real thing. The actual weight of real armour would have conditioned the way an actor moved and perhaps increased the effect of reality, although the reverse is also quite possible, which might produce the effect of comedy. I remember well one particular critic describing my final encounter between Macbeth and

Macduff in Roman Polanski's film of *Macbeth* as like 'Nervo and Knox (two much-loved variety comedians) in tin cans'.

In speaking about armour and its weight, I remember an occasion on a film location when a star (who must be nameless) complained about the weight of his expensive, specially made chain mail suit. On an extremely hot Spanish day he staggered out of his caravan, the worse one imagined for alcoholic wear and tear inside the caravan, carrying in his arms the chain mail leggings. 'Just feel the weight of this. I'm not wearing it' he said to the director, as the atmosphere on the set considerably darkened. But no one should have worried, for a potentially explosive situation was quickly saved by the director saying that he himself would wear it whilst shooting – and for as long as he could stand it, so then could the actor, who returned to his caravan duly chastened. The crew then witnessed for some time the bizarre spectacle of a knight in full chain mail suit directing the shoot.

In addition to the weight of near real armour sometimes producing a more realistic result, it provides the opportunity of greater realism in fights by

More dangerous than swords? Resting between bouts, Macbeth and Macduff enjoy cigarettes, whilst Macbeth has an injured finger attended to by the nurse.

Jon Finch as Macbeth and Terence Bayler as Macduff in Roman Polanski's film of Macbeth.

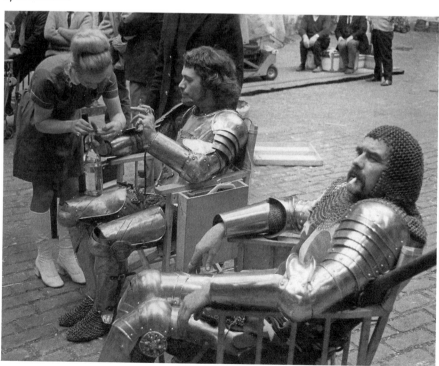

Lots of heavy contact. 'Off for more seal culling' according to the Second Assistant. Lightweight aluminium armour but still not easy to move and fight in. Launcelot meets King Arthur in the John Boorman film Excalibur. © *1981 Orion Pictures Company.*

Nigel Terry as Arthur and Nicholas Clay as Launcelot.

being able to make moves and blows safely to the body and limbs. This after all must be what happened in reality as the suit was there to protect, and furthermore it allows for greater choreographic variety than that much seen and often ridiculed blade bashing. About twenty or so years ago, fibreglass was commonly used for armour but this too had its drawbacks – a lack of convincing sound when the material was hit; also it was prone to chipping. Nowadays, we probably have available the best material ever, providing both protection and lightness, which is of course aluminium. Very easy to wear, but still metal and resembling the real thing and fairly protective, which is what armour was. There is however one problem and that is that it can *bend* and after a heavy battle scene, such as in John Boorman's Arthurian epic *Excalibur*, the blackened armourers had to work through the

Horses. The final battle. Arthur rides in with his troops in the visually stunning finale of John Boorman's film Excalibur. © 1981 Orion Pictures Company.

night hammering out the indentations, straightening the bends and put thonging back together again in preparation for the following day's excursions. The battling was indeed so heavy that our Second Assistant used to put on the call sheet 'All those concerned in the seal culling'!

Aluminium armour can also polish up to quite a shine, so much so in fact that in another film I worked on, the camera crew, whilst shooting the scene, can actually be seen mirrored on a bold knight's breastplate. There was another occasion I recall, in a Napoleonic film being shot in France, when I was forced into trying to use a car aerial as a blade substitute for a Special Effects shot, in which the blade of a sword was seen to enter the body of one of the protagonists. Hardly historically accurate, but it was the first day of shooting and our ill-prepared Special Effects man had arrived on location with the boot of his car loaded up with a motley assortment of gadgets, bits of wire, various blades, sword handles and ironmongery. When it came to doing the shot in question, not surprisingly, none of his gadgets worked. The retractable sword blade he supplied got constantly stuck and wouldn't retract as intended.

The Director went beserk for it was no way to start a film, and the shot was postponed until the next day. The following morning as dawn was breaking, I arrived on location with the Stunt Arranger and Horsemaster Richard Graydon and we noticed a strange sight. Several of the cars parked around the field where we were to shoot had lost their aerials in the night. Not slow on the uptake, we had twigged pretty quickly what had occurred and sure enough onto the set when we were about to do the 'stabbing' shot again came one red-faced, desperate-looking Special Effects man. In his hand he was carrying a sword – not exactly the same as he had supplied the day before, for into the handle was now set a car aerial for the blade. Allowing my arm to 'stand in' for the actor's, in this 'tricky' shot which demanded great accuracy, I did my very best to control the blade and stab the actor's 'opponent' in the required spot. Sadly, that aerial blade had its own ideas and a life of its own, for it wobbled and waggled high and low, all over the place. The Director now was noticeably steamed up, and I had more chance of developing my skills as a water diviner than finding the correct mark on which to land my hit and send the blade skewering into the body up to the hilt. In the end this 'sword' too had to be abandoned as was the Special Effects man who, soon after, beat a hasty retreat for England.

12.

Unarmed Combat

An admission. My own unarmed combat moves were picked up here, there and everywhere. I selected like a magpie, and still do, those which appeal to me, are useful and have about them some kind of choreographic interest. If a move is uninteresting, then I will never remember it and it doesn't get into my repertoire. I had some boxing tuition at school, purloined some wrestling moves from a couple of old professional wrestlers plus judo and aikido throws, some instruction in tai kwondo from my younger son and more recently new self-defence techniques for a play. Into this stew went some clown and commedia dell'arte techniques with some slapstick stuff and I now have something of a hotch potch of useful and appealing moves in my repertoire to call upon as needed. Many I have adapted from the real thing to make them more theatrically viable and visually exciting. Today, a trainee fight director has to undertake a more arduous and programmed course of learning which includes achieving a reasonable brown belt level in aikido or a similar unarmed martial art. There are of course so very many varied Oriental martial arts, that no one could hope to be proficient in them all, so there are always likely to be gaps in the fight directors' skills, but fortunately, so too are there gaps in plays written, requiring those same martial arts. When it comes to plays involving unusual skills and techniques which are written from time to time nowadays, such as *Punchbag* by Robert Llewellyn, which is set in a women's self-defence class, then the fight director will need to seek expert guidance. Unless, as in that case, a specific martial art technique is called for, there are a number of general movements which can be employed in a great many situations which require hand-to-hand combat or a 'punch-up', either period or modern. If a move fits the requirements of a scene, can be made to appear real, and at the same time be executed with complete safety, then it is usable. There is no particular criteria, and most movements in modern usage have been derived from wrestling, boxing, clown routines and tricks. Certain unarmed movements are of course equally useful as an ingredient in a weapon fight where the requirements are such to demand the quality that the addition of such

Unarmed combat: a kick to the face. The recipient holds his hands at chest level, one over the other, with thumbs in. The attacker is placed on a box to give height, whilst his left hand has a firm grip, which is necessary here for stability. The attacker kicks with the flat of the foot (pointing his toes). The recipient is falling backwards, in order to perform with the greatest effect, onto a mattress which protects his head from the railway line.

Jack Barry in the BBC television production of 'Night Out', an episode in the Z Cars series. Photo: Odhams Press.

moves will give. For example, in *Romeo and Juliet*, the Romeo/Tybalt encounter might well need the more desperate quality that kicks, punches and falls can give, whereas the Mercutio/Tybalt fight might perhaps be treated as a more skilled affair.

In unarmed combat, as with weapon work, success depends upon team-work and having complete confidence in your 'opponent' – which as always can only be achieved by dedicated rehearsal. Moves must be worked out with exactly the same attention paid to detail, precision, distance, rhythm and timing. When working without weapons, it should also not be thought that there is less potential danger. In fact, in my experience, there can be more possible hazard in unarmed combat, because the actors assume there to be less danger, sometimes producing a cavalier attitude and this can lead to problems. With a weapon in the hand, no one has any doubt about the technique and professionalism required. Neither should it be assumed that it is any easier setting a brawl or general rough house, although the actual blocking will probably take less time than, for example, an armed battle. Indeed, the more unruly a brawl is to appear, the more detailed it has to be. Are the actors going at it too hard for safety? Is there any furniture in the way which could prove hazardous? Is there any danger of something being knocked over which could get in someone's way or perhaps smashing (crockery, glass, etc.)? Could an actor/actress hurt themselves on that particular fall? Do they need any protection by the way of elbow, knee, back pads, etc.? Does an edge of a table need covering for safety? The list is endless and will depend on the set and the scene but the professional arranger will surely do his best to address everything.

Leaving aside for the time being the addition of any 'nasties' such as knives, scissors, bottles, pokers and other such instruments, which might in certain situations be incorporated, unarmed combat scenes will mainly be made up of slaps, punches, kicks, falls and throws and it is in this order that we shall take a look at them here. A good moment to remind the inexperienced reader that all moves should be learnt not from a book but from a qualified tutor. My intention is merely to give the learner an introduction.

Slaps

There are a variety of ways in which slaps can be effective. They will obviously be directed at the face or head and the sound of the 'connection' is usually needed in the theatre, although not in film when it can be dubbed on after. The sound is known professionally as the 'knap', and without it, the effect of the slap is lost. The audience will know it is merely a spoof. Moments of embarrassment and derision for all concerned when the blow is seen to be fake. I even once heard an entire audience groan when a punch in a big West End hit musical was seen to miss. One would have thought the arranger (as one was credited) would have changed the move, if the actors were not up to making it convincing.

There are those who in my opinion inexcusably promote the idea that a slap can actually *connect safely* with the face, providing certain procedures are observed. I have never done it and would never do it, as there is too much chance involved. Better by far to change the move, for there are always alternative possibilities. In theatre in the round, I'm afraid that tricks will be almost invariably seen, so it is on those occasions that instead of going for a connection (when the simple 'miss with sound effect approach' won't work), one should alter the move.

Now to go on to the method of the 'safe as humanly possible' technique, involving the miss and sound of the hit. The slap can be made in a number of different ways, forehand, backhand or uppercut for example, but always missing the 'opponent's' face or connecting with his waiting (not obviously) hand. The 'blow' must be ridden by the recipient, and both parties should rehearse initially quite out of distance so that the rhythm of the attack times exactly with that of his partner's head reaction. The direction of this reaction must, of course, continue in line with the 'opponent's' swing and the head should be well relaxed, for any stiffness around the neck or tension could produce injury. The preferable method is to mask the supposed moment of contact from the audience by having the recipient's back to them. If full acted intention is behind the 'blow' and the reaction is well timed and real, the audience will be convinced that they have actually witnessed the person 'receiving' being hit. Of course, in filming such blows will be carried past the face, at a height dependent upon the camera position and angle. This can sometimes depend upon the move itself and there is no need to bother about hand connections to make a sound, as this will be added in the dubbing room after.

A slap across the face inflicted by a man is essentially a follow through movement, whilst for a woman it will normally come from the elbow and stop at the cheek; but as always this is a generalisation which depends upon character and situation. There are a number of ways to make the sound effect of the 'knap' if so desired in the theatre, but fundamentally it will be produced by a connection against one's own body or that of the 'opponent' and it will be obscured from the audience. Should one be slapping with the right hand, this may be done by striking a glancing blow against one's other hand en route. Alternatively, the connection may be against one or other of the 'opponent's' hands, depending upon which hand the attacker is using to strike with. Should the attacker be using his right hand, then the recipient will *receive* with his own right hand at about breast height for the attacker to connect with in the course of his swing. This being for an upward blow and not a horizontal face slap. Alternatively, should the attacker need to use his left, then the recipient will receive with his left hand, but whichever it is, it must always be masked from the audience. If the blow is a backhander, the recipient will hold up the opposite hand to that of the attacker. Finally, the sound effect may be made by another actor on stage nearby, but the timing in this instance is extremely difficult to synchronise with the combatants' action and I would personally give it a wide berth. The slap can be made with a diagonal swing, low to high, left to right or right to left. Horizontal slaps in line with the face are a further possibility but done out of distance, striking the receiver's raised hand for the sound. The simplest method of all though for making the 'knap' is the old burlesque technique. In this case, the attacker makes his swing at the same time as his partner makes the sound of connection by slapping his own hands together. Another old comedy technique is to grab the lapel or collar of the intended victim, then open the palm of the same hand and create the slap effect by striking against the open palm. All good fun stuff! Of course whatever the method, and often this will be determined by whether the stage is proscenium, arena or in the round, the co-ordination of reaction with attack, together with the sound effect, is essential – otherwise, comedy of the wrong kind!

At the end of the day, I have to admit that slaps are not my favourite moves and I tend to avoid them whenever possible, as reliability depends upon such acute togetherness of the actors and their timing. When they go wrong, they're awful, and just silly in effect. I recall, many years ago, teaching such moves at a drama school in Denmark. A year later, I returned to view a performance in the main theatre which involved some of the same actors I had earlier trained. To my horror, I witnessed a tragedy. Although they played their combats with great élan and certainly had intention behind their moves, unfortunately all the tricks were unmasked and in full view of the audience in proper Tommy Cooper fashion. I am ashamed that the one vital instruction about *masking* cheated moves I had earlier omitted to impart, and now that Danish audience knows everything!

Punches

Punches needing the sound of contact will be facial. The most effective technique is to punch past the face with the right hand while striking one's own breast with a relaxed left hand. The correct sound in this case will not be the same as for a slap. It is much more of a 'bony' sound, and may be heard by striking the fist against the heel of the palm. It should be noted that gloved hands make a better, more realistic, noise than bare hands. The successful punch again depends upon real motivation, so that the audience sees clearly the intention from the attacker and the correct reaction from the opponent.

Punches may be made from different directions – straight right or left, roundhouse, uppercut, etc. – but essentially there are two kinds, either the jab or the follow-through. The reaction must naturally be in tune with the kind of blow received; for instance, a jab on the face will only necessitate a small recoil, whereas a full punch following through may send the recipient flying off balance. With any punch to the head, as with the slap, the head of the victim in reaction must follow the line of the punch. With punches to the body, it is most important that they are always pulled. In cases where a supposedly hard punch is seen to land in full view of the audience, some form of padding should be worn under clothing.

Body punches will nearly always require some sound, mostly vocal, taking care not to outrage probability. Remember that a hard punch to the body will force a sharp exhalation of breath rather than a shout, especially if the punch lands in the solar-plexus region. For a punch of the follow-through variety on stage the correct distance to be from the opponent is arm's length, or further. A simple way to check this in the case of the odd punch is to measure up the distance: if right-handed, with the left hand first, before letting fly with the right, and vice versa for the left-hander. This stock method will often be seen on films and television.

Kicks

As with punches, we have two kinds – follow-through or pulled. It applies equally to kicks as to punches that the recipient must know exactly where the blow will land, and the strength of the effect lies in the preparation of the kick – any connection must be light and pulled.

If the audience sees a vicious preparation, it will most certainly believe in the attack. Even more so than with punches, the attacker must always be well balanced for at the moment of striking he will be balancing upon one leg and should he have got too close to his opponent, or not near enough, the effect of the kick will be lost: it is not possible when balancing on one leg to adjust distance by swaying the body back or forward, as when punching. So the kicker must know by practice his exact position, as there is no room for manoeuvre.

Kicks that do not follow through are made with the *flat* of the foot and *pulled*. They may be made to the thigh, inside or outside, or to the hands of the recipient, when the effect is of a kick to the face.

In the case where the kick might be preceded by a run, landing at the required distance from one's opponent is even harder, and the steps must be worked out with great precision in order to land on the correct foot and at the right distance; getting too close should be avoided at all costs. A point worth mentioning is that in a general free-for-all it is not in fact necessary to make a blow connect at all in the background for the result to look credible. With a lot of movement, overturning of furniture, noise and, most of all, acting intention, a spectacle of some realism can be achieved providing that no 'misses' are in view of the audience.

Again, the attacker must always 'act' force and never really put strength into a blow. The *intention* of the preparation is what matters, together with the reaction of the receiver.

Throws and falls

Correct tumbling, rolls and falling need training and skill, but in general terms relaxation is vital. Observe how in their ordinary play young children fall frequently, and because they do not tense up, come to little harm. Some general points, however, to bear in mind on safety are:

When falling into a roll, always keep the head well tucked in to the chest. Maintain a balanced position until the last possible moment. Take care not to fall on a bony part of the body – elbows, knees and the heel of the hand being particularly susceptible to damage. There is of course no reason, provided there is adequate covering by clothes, why an actor required to fall night after night should not wear padding on knees or elbows to prevent their being hurt. For that matter, padding may be worn anywhere that will not show; don't forget though that there is nothing worse than tell-tale bulges under a close-fitting costume! One can buy elbow and knee pads from sports shops, and campers' polyurethane rolls of bedding which affords good protection can be cut up for anywhere else (hips, backs, etc.) if the budget is limited and nothing more professional (such as a jockey back pad) available.

There are a number of different techniques for usable stage throws, from a variety of positions. Some will land a person flat on the floor, while others will send him into a roll. There are hip throws, neck throws, arm throws, the famous Irish whip and body throws of all kinds, taken from different sources, but they need in all cases careful and correct tuition and are beyond the scope of any manual alone. All the moves described, with and without weapons, could be dangerous if not learnt properly under expert guidance, and in unarmed combat it must be stressed that throws are possibly the most dangerous moves for the unskilled to undertake, and should not be attempted without trained help.

Strangling

Thank goodness, not many plays call for a strangling to take place; but a few notes may be helpful to the curious, and my information comes from reliable sources! First, a premeditated killer so I'm told may employ some article to assist in his design, such as a stocking, scarf or length of rope, and he is more likely to commit the crime from behind his victim. A spur-of-the-moment killer may attempt to strangle from the front. If a ligature is used the victim's death will be quick due to stoppage of the blood-flow, rather than a fight for breath. A person who is attacked in this way, whether strangled with bare hands or with a scarf, will react more or less the same way, and there are three stages in his reaction.

1. Surprise (naturally enough!).
2. Instinctive response to defend against the attack.
3. An involuntary fight for life.

If rope, cloth or the like is used, the actor should hold on to the knot himself, leaving the ligature comfortably relaxed around the neck of the 'victim'. Any kind of pressure on the neck should obviously never be used, but rather the effect of effort can be concentrated into pressing the hands together. When the action is performed with hands alone, and the assault is from the front, the attacker should put the acted pressure into the palm of the hands, keeping the thumbs relaxed, and pretend pressing downward on the collar bone of the 'victim', and never inwards on to the neck. Whatever the case, real strength is not to be used, it must be acted.

Going on to a brief word about the use of extra props such as bottles or scissors, it is essential to use fakes rather than the real thing, even though use of the genuine article will undoubtedly foster a greater respect and regard for the possible danger of these instruments. When a substitute is used, the real article should if possible be established at some prior point in the play, in order that the audience will not question reality. Should, and I hope it never is the case that there is no alternative, the use of a real instrument be necessary, then a vital precaution is the Sellotaping of sharp edges of any article, be it the blades of scissors, a knife or a broken bottle. Personal fear when fighting with the real instrument is likely to result in loss of co-ordination and tentatively executed moves. Understandably, and apart from that, it is *dangerous*, so I cannot stress too strongly that only dummy weapons or those made safe should be used.

In conclusion, one or two very important points of a general nature.

First, *never* deviate in any way from what has been set in rehearsal.

Secondly, never strive for quantity, but rather for quality. A short, well-planned and well-executed brawl or fight is in every way preferable to a long, meaningless free-for-all.

Thirdly, when one has actually to be struck with an instrument, it is essential to pad the place to be hit, and it is naturally vital to rehearse thoroughly, so that the blow is in the same place every time.

Finally, a tip for the inexperienced, working on their first unarmed fight, is to start something going in slow motion. From this, openings will be seen, and the correct reactions become apparent – so something can then be set as a basis upon which to work – but this is for trainee fight directors. If you're professional, fringe or amateur, don't muddle along on your own. Better by far to give British Actors Equity a phone call and seek the advice of one of their registered qualified arrangers.

13.

Fight Notation & Writing It Down

Ａs yet, there is no universal system of notating a fight scene. This is a pity, for a generally accepted form would be invaluable to stage managers, actors and arrangers. Most fight directors have their own method of writing moves down, according to the way in which they work, but none covers every possible movement. In fact, it will be seen from the examples which follow that the main concern is with blade moves, but this is very limiting for in a great many situations a lot more is going on than simple sword strokes. How, for instance, does one write down 'woman hides under the table' except in long hand, or 'fighter half-turns whilst ducking, placing the left hand on the floor and extending the right to aim at the knee'? Only the Benesh system of Movement Notation would appear to cover all possibilities, and to learn it involves a three-month course.

For interest's sake, I list four different systems – John Barton's, Arthur Wise's, my own and an example of the Benesh Movement Notation as used by Bronwen Curry of the English National Ballet (formerly London Festival Ballet).

John Barton (Associate Director, Royal Shakespeare Company)

This system as devised by John Barton has the merit of being extremely clear and easy to use. The diagram shown opposite represents the body, and two diagrams are required for each phase of action, one for each of the combatant's moves. Every move is numbered according to the order in which it occurs, and is positioned on the diagram wherever the attack or parry is made on the body. The plus sign is used to indicate an attack and the minus a parry. A move of the foot is shown by the letter 'F' in brackets, with an arrow to point the direction. John Barton claims that in most cases, provided an actor remembers the main moves through having them thus recorded, the manner in which the movement is made, and subsidiary moves will also be recalled easily.

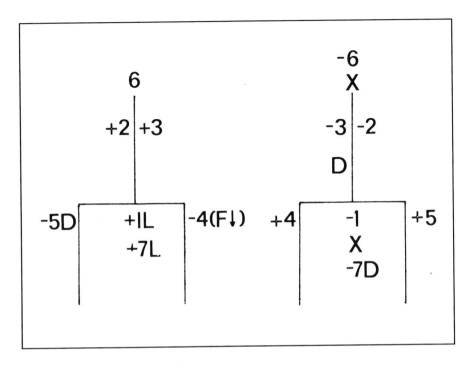

The example reads as follows:

Fighter A Lunges forward with a thrust.
Fighter B Parries down with a cross sword and dagger parry.
Fighter A Attacks to left shoulder.
Fighter B Parries.
Fighter A Attacks to right shoulder.
Fighter B Parries and replies with an attack to left flank.
Fighter A Parries taking the foot back.
Fighter B Attacks to right flank.
Fighter A Parries with the dagger and attacks to the head.
Fighter B Parries with crossed sword and dagger.
Fighter A Thrusts to waist.
Fighter B Parries with the dagger.

Arthur Wise

The basic system of Arthur Wise's notation is to separate the specific blade moves of the fighters from the more general movements over the stage area. The body is divided into various parts with each part being given a letter (A, B, C, etc.). A thrust is indicated by encircling the area aimed at, i.e. Ⓑ and a cut by a semicircle over the letter, i.e. ⌒D. The stage area is divided also into various areas to which the fighters move, so → 2 indicates a general move to area 2. Solid and open rectangles are used for movements of the feet. An example of the system looks like this:

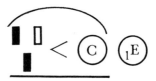

which reads:

A counter attack. The defender moves his right foot to the left, whilst attacking to area C with a thrust, and then follows this with a dagger thrust to the right side of the abdomen.

A more extensive example of the notation looks like this:

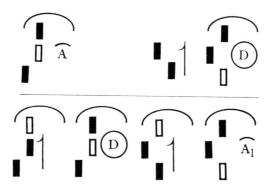

The Benesh Movement Notation

The extract opposite taken from my own sequence from the London Festival Ballet's production of *Don Quixote* was notated by Bronwen Curry FIChor, and gives a description of the body movements, stage locations, relationships of participants, identification of attacking and defending movements and exact point of blade contact.

Benesh Movement Notation was first adopted by the dance world in 1955. Today it is used by companies throughout the world for the preservation and staging of repertoires. Other applictions such as Medical Research, Social Anthropology, Work Study, Ergonomics, Gymnastics and Stage Management have received less attention.

The Benesh Institute, founded in 1963 to co-ordinate developments in all movement fields and to house a movement library, offers one full-time specialist course and a correspondence course which introduces the principles and components of BMN as a basis for specialised study.

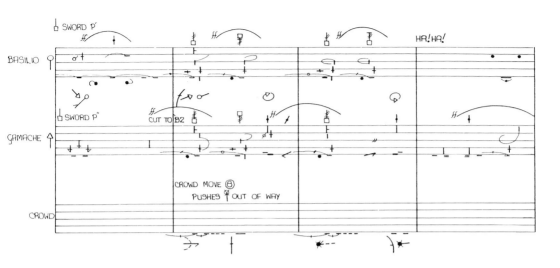

My own method

The following symbols I devised some 20-odd years ago and have to admit that I now find the method not comprehensive enough for the various permutations of moves which I employ! Also, a video recorder is faster and more accurate than any notation. The symbols for the purpose of jotting down a simple sword sequence are however satisfactory and easily learnt. Wherever possible, an attempt has been made to make the symbol suggest the movement it represents.

Thrust	•	L. flank	⅄
Head	T	Ducks	
Feints	∧	Throw	
Envelops	↩	Sidestep L.	
Sword only	⋈	Sidestep R.	
Jumps	◱	Parry and reply	
Lock	↲	Swings	
Parry	∠	Short pause	
Circle	◯	Long pause	
Lunge	—	Body to body	=
Pushes	+	Moving forward	⅄
Pulls	‡	Moving back	⋀
Kick	↳	One step forward	⋀
Kills/wounds	✳	One step back	⋁
Cut	⅄	Deceive circular parry	⊙
R. shoulder	⅄	Dagger only	↙
L. shoulder	⅄	(or any weapon in left hand)	
R. flank	⁄	Sword and dagger	✕

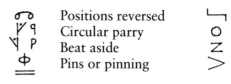

With two hands		Positions reversed	
Punches/slaps to left cheek		Circular parry	
Punches/slaps to right cheek		Beat aside	
Punches to stomach		Pins or pinning	
Stairs (or any higher level)			

Note. The parry number may be put in the symbol, i.e. ⌐4 or ⌐2. Parry 5 and reply would be ⌐5⌐, although it is, of course, clear from the attack which parry will in most cases be used. Similarly, many steps forward or back as required may be written, i.e. four steps forward would be ∕∧⅘ .

A short phase using symbols
A Cuts to right shoulder.
B Parries and envelops and replies with a thrust to right knee.
A Parries.
B Thrusts again to right knee.
A Circular parries, beating aside and replies with a cut to the head.
B Parries and cuts to left shoulder.
A Parries and kills.

A ∕⅄,   B ∠↵.∧,   A ∠,   B ∧,   A 0Z∕T,   B ∠⅄,   A ∠✳

It will be seen that although covering weapon play adequately even if in a rather limited fashion and simplistically, all the systems outlined above, except the Benesh Notation, are not designed to include unarmed combat. It is mainly blade moves that are recordable; what the body is doing whilst making these moves is left out, so there is a gap to be filled. What is needed is a very simple system, easily taught to drama students, stage managers and actors, that will cover any permutation of blade and weapon strokes, together with any possible body movement and unarmed combat whether it be a pirouette whilst making a sword swipe, hitting some poor unfortunate over the head with a tray, or putting an arm lock on an opponent before a throw. I hope it won't be too long before such a system is devised.

Description of moves

The description of moves is intentionally simple, so that those untrained, whether actors, editors, stage managers, continuity staff or directors, can clearly understand the moves in a general way. The following two examples, from the films *Flash Gordon* and *The Return of the Musketeers*, are illustrations of writing out the descriptions of moves in long hand. The routines were devised and written during the rehearsal periods and were not the final versions.

Contest Disc Fight   from *Flash Gordon*

1. Flash charge
   Barin avoid leaving Flash on edge

2. Flash charge
   Barin sidestep using right arm to avoid and block and make to kick
      Flash off edge with left foot
   Flash arm lock on Barin and pull him past to other side and punch
      (R hand) to face
   Barin blocks (1 arm) and avoids under Flash's arm, following with
      kick to stomach
   Flash falls back

3. Flash charge (Barin having moved around to his left)
   Barin sidestep and grab from behind
   Flash throws Barin over shoulder
   Barin from floor spreadeagles Flash's legs apart with own, and
      thumps to side with right arm as
   Flash attempts downward punch,
   Flash falls back

4. Barin throws himself on top of Flash (on floor)
   Flash rolls him off with right leg

5. Flash head butt to stomach
   Barin thumps down onto his back with fist
   Flash falls as
   Barin rolls over him to other side

6. Flash right arm swing to face from the floor
   Barin blocks with right hand grabbing arm and in sitting position
      pivots under Flash's arm, following with kick to chest

   ### Sword dropped in between them by Hawkman Referee

   Both go for sword, but knives appear in front of Flash and Barin
      gets the sword
   Barin backs Flash to edge and is about to thrust when knives come
      up in front of him and

   ### DISC TILTS

   Flash escapes away and Hawk Ref drops him a spear

7. Barin cuts to right shoulder
   Flash parries, envelops and thrusts with the spear
   Barin circular parry/beat aside and swing sword behind back pinning
      Flash at the edge of disc

Flash attempts move to right
Barin turning clockwise thrusts to right knee
Flash parries with spear as avoiding with right foot back, moving
    away to his left
Flash throws spear (a mistake!!)

DISC TILTS

8. Flash dive rolls for a whip which has been dropped in on the
    opposite side of disc by Hawk Ref
    Flash cracks whip at Barin's ankles
      ”   ”   ” ” ” head
    Barin lunges at Flash going past
    Flash cracks whip at Barin's right side
      ”   ”   ” ” ” head but
    Barin avoids with left foot behind as
    Flash's whip wraps around sword and he pulls Barin to him as
    Flash thumps into ribs with right elbow
    Barin falls
    Flash pulls sword off disc with whip (still wrapped around it)
    Barin barges Flash who attempts whip over back and with knee to
        stomach pushes him off
    Flash cracks whip over Barin's head
      ”   ”   ” around left leg (it winds around) – pulls it and
    unwinds Barin as

DISC TILTS

9. Flash cracks whip over Barin's head
    Flash wraps whip around Barin's waist
    Barin winds himself into Flash and punches to face, who falls off the
        disc *but* (luckily!)
    there is a whip dangling down from the Hawk Ref and Flash
        manages to catch this. He is suspended in space momentarily, and
        swings himself back onto disc with the whip in hand as

DISC TILTS

10. Flash goes on past Barin who is probably clutching hold of knives to
     stop falling off the disc
    Barin cracks whip to Flash's head
      ”   ”   ” ” ” left side moving around
    Flash cracks whip at Barin's legs
    Barin rolls out of the way and cracks whip back at the stomach as
     getting up

Flash jumps back out of the way
Barin cracks the whip out of Flash's grasp

....

11. Barin winds whip around Flash's legs, pulling him down
        ,,   cracks whip to head five times with Flash avoiding left and
    right
    Barin cracks to Flash's right (Flash still on floor)
       ,,   ,,   ,,   ,,   left
       ,,   ,,   between the legs
       ,,   ,,   twice as Flash rolls away to his left
    Barin winds whip around Flash's legs whilst Flash still on the floor
    Flash grabs hold of whip and pulls Barin to him
    They grapple on the edge
    Flash attempts to throw Barin off edge
    Barin bends Flash back over knives as

DISC TILTS

12. Barin falls/rolls down the disc grabbing hold of knives as he goes
    which (hopefully) will retract as he goes onto the next group, and
    finally he is hanging over the edge with disc at maximum tilt
    Flash throws out whip, which Barin catches hold of in the nick of time!

Raoul/Justine Fight   from *The Return of the Musketeers*

R and L directions are from the *opponent's* point of view.

   J. – Running turn back and swipes at Raoul over head
   R. – Ducks, rolls and draws sword

....

1. R. – Thrusts to R knee
   J. – Parry, feint to L shoulder
   R. – Attempt hand and sword parry
   J. – Thrust to L waist
   R. – Parry prime (wrist watch position)
   J. – Thrust to R breast
   R. – Parry, coupé (twice blade over) and thrust to R waist
   J. – Avoid (no parry) taking R foot across

....

2. J. – Thrust to R breast
   R. – High seconde parry (blade point down) and move forward to
        attack

The villainess escapes the clutches of the musketeers.

Kim Cattrall fights Michael York in Richard Lester's The Return of the Musketeers *with Oliver Reed, Frank Finlay and Thomas C. Howell in the background.*

J. – Move back and passada-soto (backward lunge) and point to R.'s
     chest
R. – Knock blade away with hand and lunge
J. – Back (avoiding) around tree and cut to R shoulder
R. – High seconde (hand high, point down) parry

....

(Raoul retreat – Justine follow)
3. R. – Falling – straighten arm
   J. – Beat blade aside (R to L) and cut to R shoulder
   R. – Parry sword and hand (shoulder parry – point up) and retreat

....

4. J. – Turn and move away
   R. – Advance
   J. – Stop him with reverse stab (change grip)
   R. – Attempt to kick blade away
   J. – Move blade away to avoid kick and again point at R.'s chest
   R. – Attempt to grab blade with hand
   J. – Again moves blade away avoiding R.'s grab, and move away
5. R. – Thrust to L shoulder
   J. – Parry, envelop (take control of blade) and thrust to L knee
   R. – Hand parry and thrust to R knee – going past J.
   J. – Parry seconde (low right) and push R. with L hand

(POSITIONS REVERSED)

J. – Follows and thrust to L waist
R. – Parry prime (wrist watch position) and reply with thrust to R
     breast
J. – Hanging parry
R. – Thrust to R knee (coupé)
J. – Parry seconde (low right) avoiding to L

....

(Justine driving Raoul back)
6. J. – Beat R.'s blade (L to R) and thrust to L waist
   R. – Prime parry (wrist watch)
        (J. forward – R. retreat)
   R. – Thrust to R waist
   J. – High seconde parry (point down) and thrust to L breast
   R. – Hand parry whilst avoiding right
        (J. move L; R. move L, J. move R)
        (J. feint, R. retreat)
   R. – Thrust to L waist

J. – Prime (wrist watch) beat aside/coupé (over blade) and thrust to R
  waist

R. – Hand parry

J. – Thrust again to R waist

R. – High seconde parry (point down) whilst avoiding L and

BACK AGAINST TREE

7. J. – Thrust to L waist

  R. – Parry prime (whilst avoiding) and cut to R shoulder
    KNOCKING OFF HAT (Justine revealed) – As

  J. – Ducks and parries (R shoulder parry)

RAOUL BACKS AWAY. JUSTINE ADVANCES

8. R. – Straighten arm

  J. – Sharp upward beat to blade
    (J. advance – R. backs)

  R. – Straighten arm

  J. – Sixte (R shoulder parry position) envelop (taking R.'s blade) and
    thrust to R knee

  R. – Circular seconde (low R pos.) parry and FALL BACK OVER
    TREE

9. J. – Holds sword at R.

  R. – Beats blade aside (L to R) and cuts to L waist

  J. – Parry (point up) and disarms R. using L hand and kick.
    – CATCHES SWORD AND POINT TO R.'s THROAT

finish

14.

Acting Intention & Acted Aggression

The word 'intention' is used by professionals to mean the acting-through during the combat of the requisite pitch of emotion and fight aggression. Often one sees fights in plays where the level of anger and aggression displayed prior to the actual set-to is not maintained during the combat. When this happens the emotional level is dropped, and consequently the effect of reality. The involvement of the audience is suspended and the illusion is lost. I remember one 'furious Tybalt' coming back again to encounter Romeo, and the savage exchange of words shifting shamelessly at the first contact to a pat-a-cake altercation – more reminiscent of the children's game than Tybalt's threat of 'bitterest gall'. The commonplace reasons why this happens are that actors are under-rehearsed or have been given over-complicated movements which are beyond their basic ability. No matter how cleverly a fight is arranged, nothing is as important as its *acting*.

In the performance of a combat two contradictory things are happening. On the one hand, *characters* are seen to be performing on a highly charged emotional level. On the other, the *actors* have to be working mentally on a conscious level of coolness, with complete body relaxation and control, so that their acted aggression can be performed with conviction, and at the same time in absolute safety. Always there is the danger that a certain type of actor wishing to 'put on a good show' may expose himself or his fellows to actual bodily harm, by over-zealously extending the acting 'intention' into real aggression. Like Hamlet when he complains of over-acting, such excess 'offends me to the soul', I too would 'have such a fellow whipped'! Such actors should be reminded that real strength or fury will not necessarily come across to an audience!

The problem lies in the actor's desire to 'look good' – the kind of person, West End star or young climber, who cares little for anything or anybody outside his own performance. Come what may, he is going to be 'wonderful'. The same kind of individual is often the sort, too, who will not listen to advice and he's then surprised, making excuses how the 'fault lies elsewhere' when there's an accident. It was a faulty sword, or the other actor came too close, or didn't do what he was meant to do, or changed a movement in midstream. I could go on, but we all know the sort. They usually make their presence felt at the very first rehearsal.

Some years ago I remember a young actor at Stratford-upon-Avon who, clad in armour and in the thick of the *Coriolanus* battle, charged shouting at his 'opponent' from the back of the steeply raked stage. In the course of the attack he slipped and went skidding on his backside right past his astonished would-be combatant, right off the stage, ending up sprawled across the lap of a bewildered spectator in the front row of the stalls – audience participation, I would say, taken to extremes! The story did not quite end there. Not only did the audience also witness the humiliating episode of the warrior scrambling ignobly back on to the stage, but also of the spectator upstaging everyone by rising from his seat and holding aloft (with certain pride) his battle-injured bloody index finger! Such an actor may feel well satisfied with his emotional involvement, but this can be dangerous, as we have seen; a cool head, technical skill and simulated emotion are far more likely to achieve the intended dramatic force of the scene.

Sequences of movements can be splendidly choreographed, and the combat devised with invention and skill, but when the acting of the fight is not at the necessary pitch of supposed aggression there will be no illusion of reality – in fact, a non-fight and this is not the same thing as outlined earlier when an actor goes about his task in an uncontrolled and heavy-handed manner. I am referring to *acted* aggression and not *real* aggression.

Naturally, there will be some situations where the characters are non-belligerent, as in the Aguecheek/Viola scene in *Twelfth Night* but in such skirmishes the moves must still be executed with the same care and intention, even allowing that they may have been selected for their apparent *lack of effort*, and the idea is to show up the ineffectualness of the characters.

On the whole, it is better to perform a shorter sequence well, and with acting intention behind the moves, than to drag out a longer routine in which performance level is under pitch, owing to actors being hesitant about their movement sequences. Complete control is the essential requirement, while an appearance is given of being out of control. A generalisation, perhaps, but in most cases true.

Many years ago, there was a production of *Hamlet* for which I had arranged the final duel with Ian McKellan and Tim Piggott-Smith as Hamlet and Laertes respectively. Over weeks of rehearsal they had worked arduously, and the result of their labours showed in breathtaking brilliance at the dress rehearsal. Unfortunately, come the First Night it was quite another case. As I watched from my hiding place at the back of the stalls, I was aware as they were approaching the duel that tension between them was mounting on that stage. I felt uneasy and sensed problems afoot. Sure enough, on the

After the duel. 'Exchange forgiveness with me noble Hamlet.' The poisoned rapier has done its work after the multi-weaponed duel in Franco Zeffirelli's film of Hamlet. © *1990 World Icon N.V.*

Mel Gibson as Hamlet and Nathaniel Parker as Laertes.

lines 'Come on Sir', 'Come my Lord', one or other (I can't remember which) made the correct attack, but with such force, coming from the nerves of an Opening night, that unfortunately the blade of the sword broke on the very first contact. In that one moment, weeks of dedicated rehearsal went down the drain, for what followed was decidedly under par and the duel lost most of its previous excitement and intensity. All due to too much force as a direct result of tension. The line between First Night nerves being under control, without losing acting intention, is a very fine one indeed.

15.

Swords – A Brief History

*P*robably the first swords to be made were fashioned from spearheads. The sword of the Bronze Age period was in reality a long knife, and because bronze is too soft to be used for blade-to-blade combat, it had to remain a thrusting weapon only, and could not be employed for cutting purposes. This 'long knife' continued to thrive in the Iron Age, when it was used against people who had no kind of armour to protect themselves. Later on, however, the Hellenes, who were possibly the first people to use a crude armour – namely shield, helmet and basic body protection – had sword edges sharpened. Thus the weapon became a cutting instrument as well as a stabbing one, able to hack through the armour of the foe. As a result the sword became broader, and therefore heavier to wield.

The use of iron swords spread across Europe, but for many centuries these swords were lacking in any form of hand protection, for the idea of parrying a cut or thrust with the sword blade had not yet arrived, due most likely to the sheer weight of the weapons. Protection of this sort did not come to Europe until about the tenth century, and at the beginning took the form of a simple cross hilt. Later on the shield was discarded in favour of a more elaborate guard for the hand, and as fighting developed into sword against sword this guard became more solid, particularly during the twelfth to fourteenth centuries.

The Middle Ages saw a diversity in the types of swords used. Broadly speaking, these could be divided into two groups: the Asiatic (Mongol, Tartar, Cossack), and the European. The former had no hand-guard to their sword at all, whereas the European fostered the guard, on the sensible principle, perhaps, that the enemy would fight back! So from the simple cross hilt of the Crusaders came a knuckle guard, and finally a fully guarded hilt. The cutting sword grew heavier and heavier until the arrival of the Italian Sciavona, which had a completely enclosed hilt; from this came the Scottish claymore of the sixteenth and seventeenth centuries, a variation of the normal Western European style. With the invention of gunpowder the armoured knight became obsolete, and with him went armour and shields.

The tendency was towards a cut-and-thrust weapon – in other words, the long, narrow-bladed rapier, the hilt of which became even more protected.

By the Elizabethan age swords were reflecting the fashion of the period, and as the blades became better forged, so they were able to be more elaborate, and became 'the badge of gentlemen'. Men-at-arms carried cruder weapons, and during peace-time they were more or less forbidden to carry arms at all in public places because it was well known that ex-soldiers all too frequently took to such professions as foot-pad and highwayman.

The swords of gentlemen continued to grow more elegant in the seventeenth and eighteenth centuries, finally evolving into the small-sword. The hilts of these times were of enamel and precious metals such as gold and silver, and the blades were made of the finest steel, and were as much a part of a gentleman's dress as his lace handkerchief. However elaborately these rapiers were decorated, they were nonetheless formidable and highly practical weapons. About the time of Marlborough's campaigns the small-sword developed into the heavier sword of the Georgian officer, the lighter weapon being ineffectual for battle. With the development of the bayonet, it was necessary for the infantry officers to have a much more robust weapon, and the cavalry sabre made its appearance. A controversy arose in the nineteenth century over whether the sabre should be used for cutting or thrusting. In the end it was used for both.

During the French Revolution the armouries of the aristocrats were looted, and the citizens paraded with priceless small-swords. When it came to a set-to, however, they preferred to use the broad-bladed sabres with heavy curves, being completely untrained in the use of these other weapons. In the revolutionary army the rule was, the more important the officer (in his own estimation, at least!), the bigger the sword.

In the period after Waterloo, when British officers became very dandified, the dress or 'walking' sword became lighter and very thin-bladed, and of such length that it could be carried over the left arm – or alternatively allowed to drag on the ground! It wasn't very long after this that swords were abandoned as weapons of war, and the only serious use they have today is as bayonets used mainly as stabbing instruments – very much akin, in fact, to the first use for which they were made thousands of years ago!

Introductory note to sword illustrations

The weapons illustrated are a fair selection of those that can be easily hired or still bought on the open market. They are historically authentic in essence, but necessary adaptations have been made for use on stage.

A 1 Roman sword
  2 Greek sword
  3 Egyptian sword
  4 French military side-arm, 1820s
    (to be found in majority of
    theatrical armouries and used as
    Roman swords for stage purpose)
  5 Roman short-sword

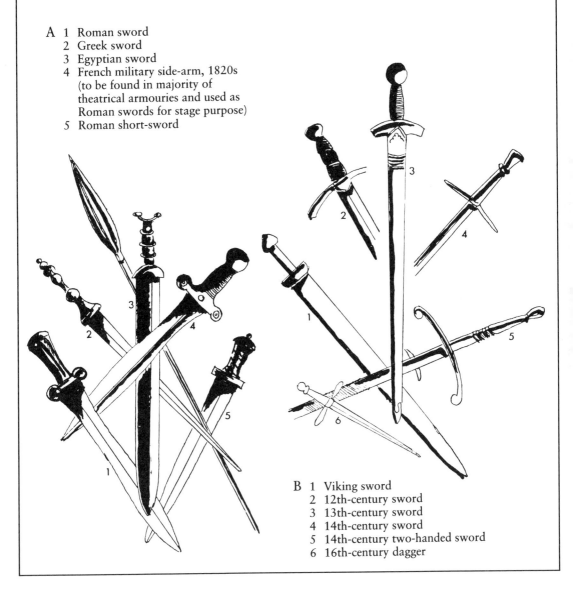

B 1 Viking sword
  2 12th-century sword
  3 13th-century sword
  4 14th-century sword
  5 14th-century two-handed sword
  6 16th-century dagger

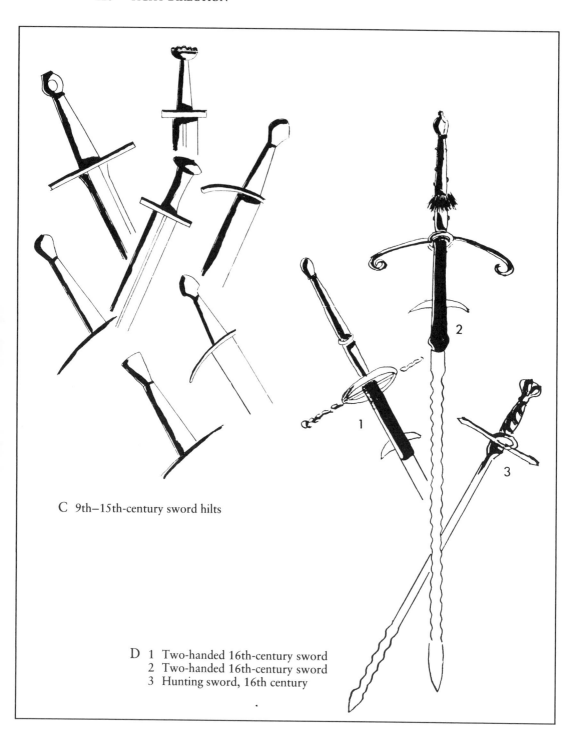

C 9th–15th-century sword hilts

D 1 Two-handed 16th-century sword
  2 Two-handed 16th-century sword
  3 Hunting sword, 16th century

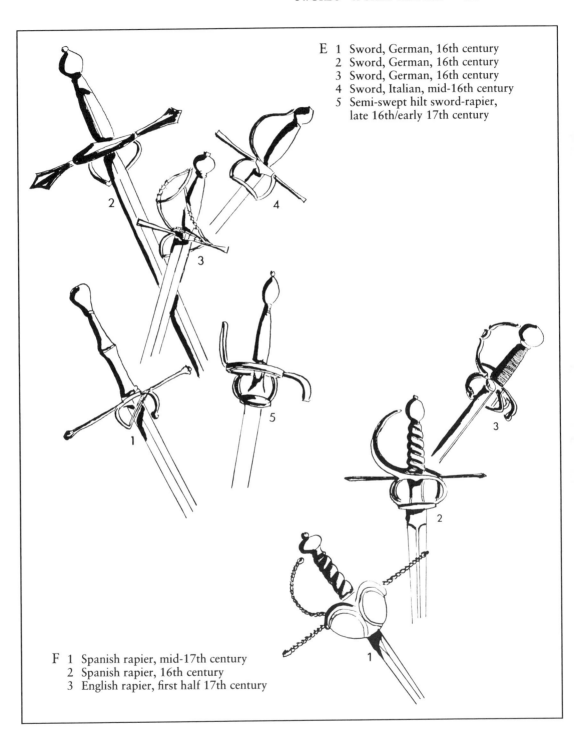

E 1 Sword, German, 16th century
  2 Sword, German, 16th century
  3 Sword, German, 16th century
  4 Sword, Italian, mid-16th century
  5 Semi-swept hilt sword-rapier,
    late 16th/early 17th century

F 1 Spanish rapier, mid-17th century
  2 Spanish rapier, 16th century
  3 English rapier, first half 17th century

G 1 *Main-gauche* dagger, Spanish, first half 17th century
2 Sword-rapier, 17th century
3 Spanish cup-hilt rapier, first half 17th century
4 Swept-hilt sword-rapier, early 17th century
5 *Main-gauche* dagger, first half 17th century

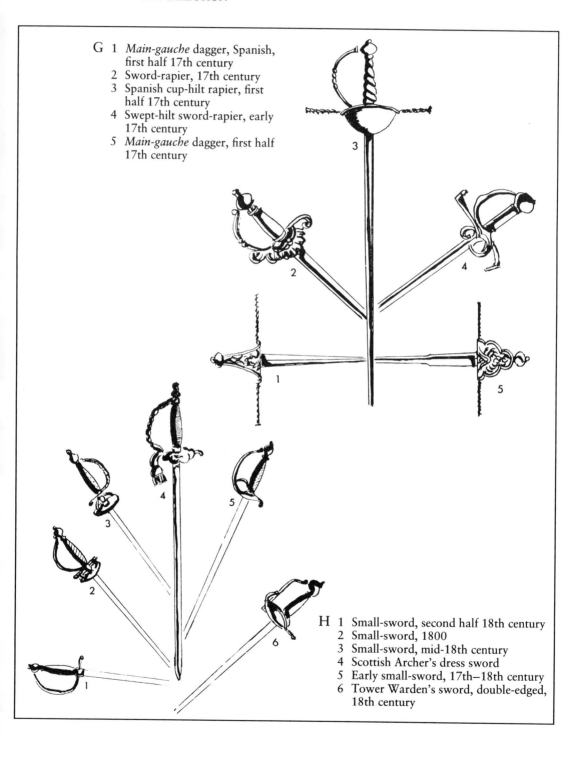

H 1 Small-sword, second half 18th century
2 Small-sword, 1800
3 Small-sword, mid-18th century
4 Scottish Archer's dress sword
5 Early small-sword, 17th–18th century
6 Tower Warden's sword, double-edged, 18th century

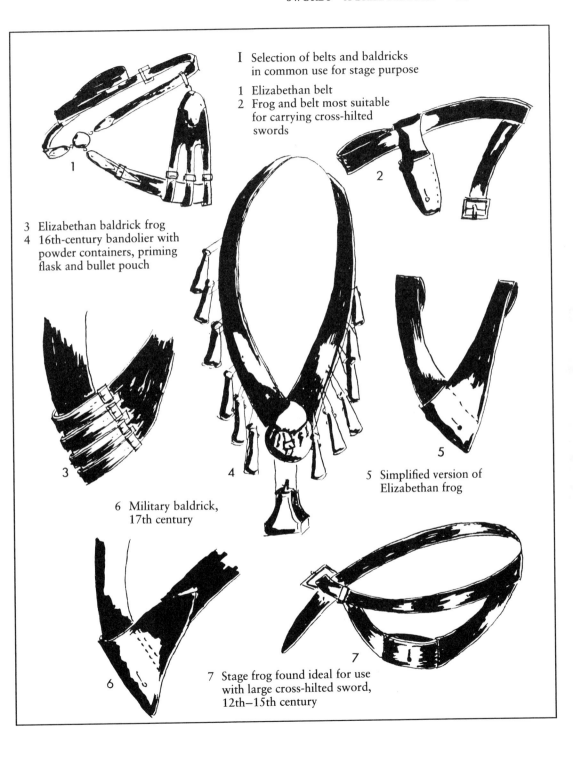

I Selection of belts and baldricks
  in common use for stage purpose

1 Elizabethan belt
2 Frog and belt most suitable
  for carrying cross-hilted
  swords

3 Elizabethan baldrick frog
4 16th-century bandolier with
  powder containers, priming
  flask and bullet pouch

5 Simplified version of
  Elizabethan frog

6 Military baldrick,
  17th century

7 Stage frog found ideal for use
  with large cross-hilted sword,
  12th–15th century

J 1 Balkan Yatagen dagger
  2 Kukri dagger
  3 Cossack dagger, Kindjal
  4 Japanese short-sword, Wakizashi
  5 Indian dagger, Kard
  6 Burmese Dha dagger

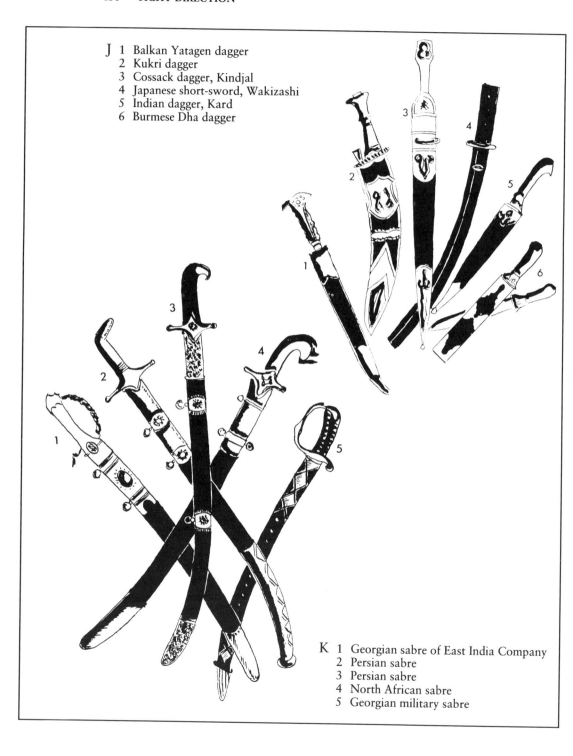

K 1 Georgian sabre of East India Company
  2 Persian sabre
  3 Persian sabre
  4 North African sabre
  5 Georgian military sabre

16.

General Information

Staged deaths

There are a great many moves, both armed and unarmed, which can be used convincingly on stage to depict a death, ranging from a faked blow to the head to a 'mortal' sword-thrust.

A credible result depends on acting intention on the part of the attacker, and the reaction of the victim. With swords, the killing stroke usually needs at the right moment to be masked from the audience. It is a case of the quickness of the hand deceiving the eye. Technique plus trickery!

Use of blood

There are some occasions when the use of blood is a necessity, and indeed the text of certain scenes, such as the murder of Julius Caesar, demands it. However, it is surprising how rare such demands are, for most injuries and woundings can be presented without blood and gore. It is not the fact that a person bleeds from a wound which affects an audience, but rather how an attacker and victim react. As a shock measure stage blood can be effective in appropriate situations, but in many cases the sight of an oozing red liquid is unnecessary, and can indeed hamper belief, rather than add to it.

There are three types of theatrical blood:
1. Stage Blood, which is slow running (but very red).
2. General Purpose Blood, which is normal consistency (i.e. fairly red).
3. Blood Capsules, which contain a powder pigment and are for use in the mouth only (but, from experience, revolting to use). (See List of Suppliers.)

plus
Real Blood (expensive)!

Swords

If a sword, or particularly a dagger, does not have to be drawn, it should be fastened to the scabbard or frog to ensure that it will not fall out.

When the historically correct sword-guard is very elaborate, or the cross bar has a pronounced downward curve, it is sometimes necessary to compromise in style; for there is a danger when fighting of the opposing blade becoming trapped in the guard. It goes without saying that care should be taken in selecting weapons, to choose those which are at the same time usable by the actors as well as being correct for period and character.

Care of weapons

Regular care of fighting weapons is essential. For instance, a loose hilt could prove dangerous by upsetting the balance of the sword at a vital moment. It is important also to inspect swords before each performance for notches in the blade. They often occur after use, and should be filed down to avoid gashed hands. If a blade becomes so badly notched as to necessitate being ground on a grindstone, it should never be allowed to overheat, as much of the temper may be lost. Rusted blades should be treated with anti-rust oil, and the oil allowed to penetrate before using abrasives. Very worn emery cloth is an ideal rust-remover and polisher; new ones tend to scratch the blade. The edges and point of a blade should never be left sharp. Edges should be blunt, and the point rounded off. Once, unbelievably, there was a well-known theatrical hire firm which sent out swords for use with sharply pointed and dangerous blades. Even a blunt weapon in the wrong hands can be dangerous, and to work with sharp blades is potentially lethal. When I expressed my concern, I was given the surly reply by the armourer 'Well, they're only bloody actors aren't they?'!

Belts and frogs

The right type of sword belt and frog (the attachment on the belt for carrying the scabbard and sword, see illustrations on p. 129) play a vital part in helping the actor to carry the sword in the right position for both movement and ease of drawing. The shape of the sword hilt is the deciding factor. For example, the Elizabethan hilt (which is either a cup or a swept hilt) cannot have close contact with the hip, and will therefore always hang low and at an angle. The cross-hilt sword, on the other hand, was carried close to the body, and in the majority of cases vertically.

Sword frogs through the ages have altered very little except in the Elizabethan period. The modern soldier's bayonet frog is indeed more or less the same shape which has carried swords through the ages. It may be noted that although invaluable as a guide, paintings depicting sword belts can be very impractical when copied for actual stage use, for some of the fussy strappings can impede movement and usage.

The glamour of filming! The film crew waits for sufficient light to shoot the action on a rainy and gloomy Irish day. © 1981 Orion Pictures Company

School plays

A Drama Teacher, untrained in stage combat techniques and planning a fight sequence for the school play, worries me greatly. The likelihood of placing children and young people into potential danger is considerable and, if allowed, is irresponsible. 'A little knowledge . . .' as the well-known saying goes! So what should be done? If the budget won't stand even a token fee to call in expert help, then probably the only sensible advice I can give is to mime the fight.

Guns

N.B. Licences for firearms *must* be obtained from the local police station. It is not necessary for the actor using the firearm to obtain a licence, but rather the stage manager or person in charge. Licences are issued entirely at the discretion of the police, and are not obtainable for any fully automatic weapons (i.e. sub-machine-guns or machine pistols).

Points to remember

1. Even though only blanks are used, one should never on any account aim directly at anyone, because burns can still be inflicted. A safe distance to fire from is not less than four metres (about twelve feet) away from the victim. An actor being shot needs to contrive that at the moment of the shooting his hands are not in front of his body, again because of the danger of burns, even though the shot is aimed away.

2. With shotguns of the muzzle-loading variety particular care needs to be taken and the aim should be completely away from the target person.

3. If it is necessary for a gun to be fired at very close range, it is possible to hire specially prepared weapons which have the blast directed away from where one is aiming, either down or to the side. On this question of hiring, it is also possible to hire fake silencers, for a blank cannot be fired through a real silencer.

4. An actor should not necessarily react to being 'shot' by a small pistol or firearm merely by dropping inert to the floor. The weapon itself may be small, but this need not entail a small reaction. A lifelike reaction will depend upon the calibre of the gun, and whereabouts on the body the bullet is supposed to have struck. Once again, don't try to go it alone; if uncertain, call an expert in.

17.

Fight Clichés

To conclude, a light-hearted reminder of some of the more obvious fight clichés. In commemoration of past heroes of the blade, some of their once original ploys may be worthy of a second look. I do not advocate their re-use, or yet that they remain but glorious memories: only the actual situation can dictate what should or should not be used. Nowadays most of these tricks could be classified under the heading 'the art of coarse fighting', so the reader would be well advised to think again before using any in a serious combat situation.

1. The hilt-to-hilt lock, face to face, prior to push-away (a moment for dialogue in those splendid Flynn/Fairbanks films).
2. The flamboyant disarm.
3. The sword-thrust which just misses the opponent with the quivering blade becoming impaled in some object, making withdrawal impossible.
4. The killing thrust which goes under the arm, with the sword held grimly as if glued in position.
5. The blow, punch, kick which has no effect (all those Hollywood Westerns) – the receiver merely dusting himself down and fighting on apparently unharmed in super-human fashion.
6. The famous slicing of the candles, in various permutations.
7. The regulation jump over the opponent's blade.
8. All slashing away up and down stairways.
9. The sword gets stuck in the scabbard when an attempt is made to draw (humorous!).
10. The foot placed on the opponent's blade, as an aid to dialogue or for a disarm.

Close observers of my work may impertinently like to add to this list. On the rack, I'd be bound to confess to a certain relish for favourite moves; of course, these are used sparingly and selectively, but if on rare occasions Romeo, Hamlet and Macbeth have all three strangely favoured my 'golf

Combatants of supposed equality: this is the type of cliché lock position which one thinks of being accompanied by a line of dialogue, such as the 'You've come to Sherwood once too often' variety!

Matheson Lang as Romeo fights with Halliwell Hobbs as Tybalt, in Romeo and Juliet, *Lyceum Theatre, 1908.*

swing' with the hilt, let me put it down to their intrinsic skill and not my own lack of innovation, for after all, if a movement is right for a particular character and a particular weapon, that is what matters! As their creator himself so aptly put it, 'suit the action to the word, the word to the action'.

In Brief

From *Honourable Beast, a Posthumous Autobiography* of John Dexter

13 September 1979
Memo to Tony Bliss re *Mahagonny* Fight Director.

With reference to the attached memo, may I ask you to reconsider? Whilst an ex-boxer may be able to stage a 'slogging match', without a professional fight director's guidance this will, I know, lead to serious accidents, and whilst Alaska Wolf Joe (Richard Cassilly) is supposed to be killed at the end of the fight, I would hate to see Plishka laid out on our stage. I would not like to accept responsibility for a fight staged by an amateur.

Last Word

*I*t seems appropriate to finish with a Roy Kinnear story. Much loved and much missed, his quick wit was renowned. Working on the sequel to Richard Lester's *Musketeer* movies, some sixteen years after making *The Three* and *Four Musketeers*, Roy and I were standing together as the same star actors as in the earlier films appeared on set for the first time again, in apparently the same costumes. Sixteen years is a long time.

I said to Roy 'It's really weird seeing the same people in the same costumes after so long' to which he immediately dead-panned 'The weird thing is that everyone's still available.'

List of Suppliers

UK

Swords, weapons, armoury
Arms and Archery
The Coach House
London Road
Ware
Herts. SG12 9QU
Tel. 01920-460335
Fax. 01920-461044

Weapons, props, etc.
Bapty & Co. Ltd
703 Harrow Road
London NW10 5NY
Tel. 0181-969 6671
Fax. 0181-960 1106

*Stage blood, blood mouth capsules,
Kryolan washable liquid, casualty
simulation liquid*
Charles Fox Ltd
22 Tavistock Street
Covent Garden
London WC2E 7PY
Tel. 0171-240 3111
Fax. 0171-379 3401

Swords
Alan Meek
180 Frog Grove Lane
Wood Street Village
Guildford
Surrey GU3 3HD
Tel. 01483-234084
Fax. 01483-236684

USA

Swords, weaponry
American Fencer's Supply
1180 Folsom Street
San Francisco, CA. 94103
Tel. 415-863 7911
Fax. 415-431 4931

*Sport fencing equipment, some
period arms*
Santelli. Inc.
465 South Dean Street
Englewood, NJ 07631
Tel. 201-871 3105

Stage blood, breakaway bottles
Alcone Co. Inc.
5-49 49th Avenue
Long Island City, NY. 11101
Tel. 718-361 8373

List of Addresses

UK

British Actors' Equity Association
Guild House
Upper St Martin's Lane,
London WC2H 9EG
Tel. 0171-379 6000

The Benesh Institute
12 Lisson Grove
London NW1 6TS
Tel. 0171-258 3041

USA

Society of American Fight Directors
1834 Camp Avenue
Rockford
IL. 61103
Tel. 800-659 6579

Index